Dedication

Back in 1956 I was the guest speaker for a church in Boston, Massachusetts, and felt led to preach a message on giving your life to Jesus for full time service. A young woman came forward for prayer. I asked her what she wanted to do with her life. She said, "I want to be a missionary." That young woman, Jeanne DiPietro, became my wife. Since June 25, 1960, we have been serving the Lord together. Jeanne generates faith and courage wherever she goes. She has been a devoted wife. This book is dedicated to her.

A Leaf in the Wind

George DeTellis

New Missions
P. O. Box 2727
Orlando, Florida 32802

Cover Design: New Eden Graphics

A Leaf in the Wind
Copyright © 2000 George DeTellis

Published by New Missions
P. O. Box 2727
Orlando, Florida 32802

ISBN 0-9653234-3-9

Printed in the United States of America.

Contents

Introduction

One beautiful fall day when I was out of Haiti and visiting New England, I sat on the bench swing on the front porch of the home we then had on Einhorn Road in Worcester. This was a favorite place to reflect and rejuvenate from the rigors of living in Haiti. The leaves of the trees had turned into the brilliant colors of red, orange, yellow and brown. Suddenly a breeze began and quickly turned into a wind tunnel swirling around like a miniature tornado. The fallen leaves fluttered and swirled in a circle. One leaf became caught in the wind and was carried high aloft. The leaf was being tossed about effortlessly, floating first in one direction and then another. I watched it for what seemed a long time and wondered where it would land. Time and again when I thought it would settle down it was off again. It was at the mercy of the wind, when suddenly the swirling stopped and there before me the leaf settled to the ground.

Jesus when talking with Nicodemus in John the 3rd chapter said, "The wind blows where it wishes, you hear the sound of it, but cannot tell where it comes from and where it goes. So is everyone who is born of the Spirit." One of the symbols of the Holy Spirit is wind. The Greek word is *pneuma*. When the Holy Spirit fills our lives He directs our ways. We often do not know where He will lead us or how He will bring it about. And He often leads us where we would not choose to go.

My wife Jeanne and I have a theme song for our lives. We learned the song when attending a chapel service at Assumption College. It goes:

Lead us on oh Lord
Lead us on
Lead us where we dare not go

Lead us on oh Lord
Lead us on
Be with us as we face new days

My life has been a leaf caught up by the wind of the Holy Spirit. Since the day I came to faith in Jesus, I have sensed the providence of God. There was never any forethought on where I was to go to school, the churches I pastored, the Jesus People movement or the evangelistic services held around New England. God always worked the circumstances to bring me where He wanted me to be. This was certainly true of going to Haiti. The choice to go to Haiti was so out of my control that when people have asked me how I got to Haiti, I answer, "I don't know." I can only say with Paul the Apostle, "The sons of God are led by the Spirit of God" (Romans 8:14).

Understanding the Law of God

The law was given by Moses as recorded in Exodus 20. The law is holy. It is a reflection of the nature of God. The problem with the law lies with man, and it is our human nature. When we want to do good, evil is present. Paul says, "For the good that I will to do, I do not do; but the evil I will not to do, that I practice" (Romans 7: 19). Human nature is such that man is morally too weak to keep the law.

Free from the law. A Christian is a man or woman who has entered into Jesus Christ. The result is freedom from the law. The law was an instrument to bring us to Christ. It is likened to a schoolmaster or tutor (Galatians 3:24). Think of a schoolteacher with many class rules: "Do not talk, do not cheat, no gum chewing, all homework must be turned in at first period." Upon each failure, the child was scolded and a ruler put to her or his hands. Strict conformity to the rules was enforced.

The children thought, "Is there no way for me to get out of this class?" One day, someone from outside made a small hole in the back of the room. "Pssst. Come," a voice called. Some of the children sneaked out the hole. They were found in the school yard rejoicing. Jesus made the hole and He is the hole. He is the end of the law for righteousness to everyone who believes (Romans 10:4). As believers in Jesus we are free from the law. The keeping of the law of the Old Testament is not the way of attaining a right relationship with God. Right standing comes only by personal faith in Jesus Christ. Salvation is a gift of God (Titus 3:5).

Are we as Christians above the law? The moral law of the universe prevails. There are standards to which we must conform. All cannot be subjective. Not everything can be left to interpretation. Some objectivity is necessary. It is not enough to say, "Be good." People need signposts to guide them along the way. "Keep off the grass" is easily understood.

---

*People need signposts to guide
them along the way.*

The successful, the powerful, the famous or the rich are not above the law. King David thought he could write his own code. Ahab pouted over Naboth's land and finally took it by force. Jezebel got it for him. "You are the King," she said. His days ended violently with the dogs licking his blood. Prophet, preacher, politician, singer, or entertainer, regardless to what height we might rise, we are not above the law.

As believers, we are governed by the Holy Spirit. Love your neighbor and you will have fulfilled the law. We are a new creation (Galatians 6:15). It is this that the world needs to see. We are not under the law, yet not above the law.

The keeping of the law of the Old Testament is not the way of attaining a right relationship with God. Right standing comes only by personal faith in Jesus Chris. Salvation is a gift of God (Titus 3:5).

Without law. Some people have little or no knowledge of God. Children often grow up with a lack of discipline in the home. Families are fragmented. The moorings of life are absent. They do what pleases or what seems right in their own eyes. Our society is becoming more violent. Crime abounds. Our jails are full. The general public lives in fear. A society where many live without law, without moral guidelines will begin to come apart.

But he who looks into the perfect law of liberty and continues in it, and is not a forgetful hearer but a doer of the work, this one will be blessed in what he does (James 1:25).

Help Me, Lord, to Understand

When I was pastor in Worcester, Massachusetts, a beautiful young woman named Lynn came down with sugar diabetes. She eventually went blind. In my humanness I said, "I don't understand."

I know God. I have come to know Him in the person of His Son Jesus Christ. The Scriptures reveal to us His nature and His ways. I'm glad for what I know; yet much remains to be seen. Paul said, "For now we see in a mirror, dimly, but then face to face" (1 Corinthians 13:12).

———————

Some things remain to faith.
We believe where we do not know.

———————

Some things remain to faith. We believe where we do not know. Even the great tenets of our faith cannot be fathomed with our human mind. Who can understand the incarnation, the crucifixion or the resurrection? Yet, I believe these to be true.

Abraham, I'm sure, did not understand why God asked him to sacrifice his son on Mount Moriah, and yet he trusted. Job was surely confused. He was a good man, and in a short time, all was taken away from him. His children, his animals, his home and his honor were gone. Bewildered, he exclaimed, "Though He slay me, yet will I trust Him (Job 13:15).

No doubt there are personal things in your life that you do not understand which are beyond your control. We now see through the eye of faith. One day we shall know even as we are known (1 Corinthians 13:12).

For now we see in a mirror, dimly, but then face to face. Now I know in part, but then I shall know just as I also am known (1 Corinthians 13:12).

Remember to Worship

All believers are priests. Revelation 1:6 says, "and has made us kings and priests to His God and Father...""...you are...a royal priesthood" (1 Peter 2:9). As priests we are to offer up sacrifices of praise to our God.

We are to offer up sacrifices of praise to God.

Israel experienced a great deliverance from Egypt and remembered to praise the Lord. We know what God has done for us in Christ Jesus! Worship and praise naturally burst forth from our hearts to our Savior.

Remember:

Worship pleases God.

Worship elevates man into God's presence.

Worship brings heaven to earth.

The angels worship in heaven, redeemed men praise

God on the earth.

Let us praise Him with our lips, in silence, in song, music and dance. Our substance, our service, our very lives, so conducted, are a chorus of praise.

Let everything that has breath praise the Lord. Praise the Lord! (Psalm 150:6).

A Lamb for All People

John the Baptist was a voice crying in the wilderness. He prepared the way for Jesus to come by calling the nation of Israel to repent.

John preached in the wilderness and baptized in the River Jordan. His message was, "It is He who, coming after me, is preferred before me, whose sandal strap I am not worthy to loose" (John 1:27).

In the Old Testament a lamb was offered as a sin offering. A lamb is a helpless animal. It has no fangs or claws. It is not especially swift. A lamb has no means of protecting itself. It is a defenseless and harmless creature. When John saw Jesus, he declared, "Behold! The Lamb of God who takes away the sin of the world!" (John 1:29).

All people are invited to believe and be saved: all the peoples of the earth, the United States, Haiti, Europe, Asia, and Africa. From the greatest to the least, all are equally invited to come. Salvation is for all men. Jesus has died for the sins of the whole world.

Salvation is for all men.

...saying with a loud voice: "Worthy is the Lamb who was slain to receive power and riches and wisdom and strength and honor and glory and blessing!" (Revelation 5:12).

We Are Not Grasshoppers

*F*or 400 years the Hebrews were slaves in Egypt. Now they were free. Moses led them out of Egypt to the border of the Promised Land. This was the land God had given to Abraham, the father of the Jewish people.

Before entering the land, Moses sent 12 spies to inform him regarding the people, cities and conditions that existed in Canaan. Two men returned, Caleb and Joshua, and said, "Let us go up at once and take possession, for we are well able to overcome it." However, the other 10 men discouraged the people. "We are not able to go up against the people, for they are stronger than we" (Numbers 13:30, 31).

Then they said something very significant. Verse 33 reads: "...we were like grasshoppers in our own sight, and so we were in their sight."

How we see ourselves is how others will see us.

Before we look at the task that God has called us to, we must see God. We need to see God in His greatness and goodness. We need to see ourselves as God sees us—righteous and sanctified and empowered by the Holy Spirit. When we see ourselves as God sees us, we will be ready for any task He calls us to perform.

Gideon was a farmer winnowing his wheat. He was hiding from the Midianites. The angel of the Lord appeared to him and said, "The Lord is with you, you mighty man of valor!" (Judges 6:12).

What are we? We are not grasshoppers. We are mighty men of valor.

Yet in all these things we are more than conquerors through Him who loved us (Romans 8:37).

What Are You?

God expresses Himself through His creation and His creatures. "The heavens declare the glory of God, and the firmament shows His handiwork" (Psalm 19:1). God is at work in the world.

The Scriptures tell us that we are His ambassadors. The ministry of reconciliation has been passed on to us. We are the light of the world. We are the salt of the earth. We are the body of Christ.

In what way does God especially work through you? Are you the eyes of God? Reporters have been called the eyes of the world. They do not call to action, but rather report what they see. Without them, much evil and injustice would go unknown. Today with modern technology they are the instant eyes to report to the world.

Missionaries are often reported to be the feet of God (Romans 10:15).

"Hear the Word of the Lord," Old Testament prophets proclaimed. New Testament preachers are the oracles, the voice of God.

Throughout my ministry I have looked to see the hand of God. In Daniel, a hand wrote on a wall. The law was written by the finger of God.

We are sent forth in the world to set in order, repair, and build. When I first saw the bridge spanning San Francisco Bay, I said, "Only God could have built this." At New Missions, 44 buildings have gone up, built by the hand of God. Some consider MacArthur in the Pacific and Eisenhower in Europe to have been the hand of God. Are you His hand?

Some, no doubt, are His mind. Individuals given to serious thought who again, in each generation, interpret the Scriptures so that the message of God can be proclaimed to each succeeding generation. We call these people theologians.

Others are the heart of God. God is love, and His love is to be expressed to all. God is looking for men and women willing to be His heart.

———————— ✖✖✖ ————————

Each of us has our place in the body of Christ.

———————— ✖✖✖ ————————

God is alive in the world. Paul said, "For me to live is Christ." God works through His people to make Himself known.

For as we have many members in one body, but all the members do not have the same function, so we, being many, are one body in Christ, and individually members of one another (Romans 12:4,5).

A Good Servant

A kingdom parable is given in Matthew 25:14 which tells of a man who left his estate in the hands of his servants while he went to another country. The affairs of the estate were measured in talents and parceled out. One servant received five talents, another two, and the last, one.

To be a good servant one must know his Master. With our thinking and reasoning faculties, we cannot come to know God. Paul said, "But the natural man does not receive the things of the Spirit of God, for they are foolishness to him, nor can he know them, because they are spiritually discerned" (1Corinthians 2:14).

We come to know God by a personal experience. When we receive Jesus as our Savior, the Holy Spirit comes into our lives. I personally did not come to faith by someone proving to me the truth of Christianity. One night, alone in my home, I had a personal experience with God. That night, I came to know my Master.

"The Spirit Himself bears witness with our spirit that we are children of God..." (Romans 8:16). This is all the proof we need for the existence of God.

Our relationship with our Master must be maintained. Our new life began in the Spirit. Do we now grow by logic and reason? Yes, we need to grow in knowledge, understanding, and Christian service, yet always endeavoring to grow in life in the Spirit. The Christian life is first and foremost a relational experience. "...our fellowship is with the Father and with His Son Jesus Christ" (1 John 1:3).

Daily getting alone with God and a devotional reading of the Scriptures are essential to maintain a dynamic Christian life. Any relationship needs time and communication. We need to experience and enjoy the presence of God throughout our life.

We serve our Master. All of us are given resources and abilities, "our talents," with which to serve the Lord. To know God is to love Him and to love Him is to serve Him. Our Master has gone to a far country. He will return. Upon His return, He will require that we give an account of our lives, resources, and abilities and how we used them while here on earth. God is looking for a return on His investment.

God is looking for a return on His investment.

To those who have much, more will be given. And to those who have not, the little they have will be taken away and given to another.

Moreover it is required in stewards that one be found faithful (1 Corinthians 4:2).

His lord said to him, "Well done, good and faithful servant; you were faithful over a few things, I will make you ruler over many things. Enter into the joy of your lord (Matthew 25:21).

My Lazarus at the Gate

"Did you hear that Toma was struck by a car and killed?" a Haitian man asked me. "Yes," I said, "I heard that he went home to be with the Lord." "He was your Lazarus, was he not? Do you know the story of Lazarus and the rich man in the Bible?" the man asked.

All of this took place where the dirt road that leads to our mission reaches the highway. Here Toma commonly spent time. To the locals he was considered "crazy." He was always barefoot, dressed in rags, and smelly dirty. Toma was a young man, perhaps 30 years of age. He often walked down the highway, in the middle of the road, mumbling to himself. Many times when I was driving he obstructed my path, especially when another vehicle was coming.

God spoke to me one day and said, "Toma is your Lazarus at the gate. Take care of him." After that whenever I saw Toma at the end of the dirt road, I would stop and have a gift for him, or perhaps money to buy what he needed. This went on for a long time. It was one of the ministries God had personally given to me. To me Toma was a sacred trust from God. I believe that God places a Lazarus in each of our lives.

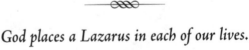

God places a Lazarus in each of our lives.

…But he who has mercy on the poor, happy is he (Proverbs 14:21).

I Was Provoked

I was provoked! A poster had irked me.

While in an agency that distributes food in Haiti, I read a poster on the wall. It said, "Jesus did not come to change a world full of hunger and suffering, but to fill it with His presence."

The poster expressed a truth, but only a half-truth.

I thought of the three Hebrew children, Shadrach, Meshach and Abednego, in the third chapter of Daniel. Because of their refusal to worship the golden image that King Nebuchadnezzar built, they were cast into the fiery furnace.

When the King later looked into the furnace, he saw not only the three walking about in the fire, but also a fourth likened to the Son of God.

In the midst of life, in every situation, God is with us. He was in the fire. Jesus said, "I am with you always, even to the end of the age."

God's presence provides comfort and assurance. His grace is sufficient. God is with you in every life situation. When in want, sickness, loneliness, discouragement, He is there.

However, Jesus did not come and die on a cross just to assure us of His presence. He came to deliver the world from sin and every form of oppression.

Nebuchadnezzar went near the mouth of the furnace and spoke, saying

> *...Shadrach, Meshach and Abednego, servants of the most high God. Come out and come here.*

The three Hebrew children came out from the midst of the fire.

God sent His Son to deliver us. We are delivered from sin and every form of evil by which the devil shows himself. Hunger, super-stition, ignorance, disease, and oppression are expressions of evil. Jesus has come to destroy the works of the devil. God is a Deliverer.

Hunger, superstition, ignorance, disease, and oppression are expressions of evil.

Haiti is being delivered from the hands of the enemy. We all need to ask God to work deliverance into every area of our lives.

God does not only grace hunger and suffering with His pres-ence. He delivers men, women and children from it.

Not even the smell of smoke was on Shadrach, Meshach and Abednego when they came out from the fiery furnace.

...I am with you always, even to the end of the age (Matthew 28:20).

God, Angry with David

Why did David invoke the anger of the Lord? He knew God and His ways. David was to have his trust in the Lord, not in the number of troops he could assemble in the event of an enemy attack.

David numbered Israel in 1 Chronicles 21. God was angry. He spoke through the prophet Gad: "Choose three years of famine, three months destroyed by your enemies, or three days of the sword of the Lord."

David answered, "Let me fall into the hands of the Lord for His mercy is great." The Lord sent a plague and 70,000 died. The angel of the Lord with his sword drawn entered Jerusalem and began destroying the city.

People at the height of success often experience their greatest failures. Some call it a death wish. As a boy, I had another boy say to me, "The best fun of building sand castles is knocking them down after they are built."

Some people are given to self-destruction. The alcoholic, the drug addict, the criminal, the gambler—they all self-destruct.

We as believers are heirs of eternal life. We are destined for greatness, not failure. In Christ, we go from victory to victory.

Angels were created to work for us, not against us. "Are they not all ministering spirits sent forth for those who will inherit salvation?" (Hebrews 1:14).

When Joshua went to fight against Jericho, an angel met him. The angel said,

"*...as Commander of the army of the Lord, I have now come*" (Joshua 5:14).

Often when in need, I have prayed, "Lord, send an angel." Amazing victory and strength have always followed.

So long as our trust and confidence is in the Lord, we will have victory. Paul said, "Yet in all these things we are more than conquerors through Him who loved us (Romans 8:37).

We will have victory.

David called upon the Lord and offered up sacrifice. The angel of the Lord put his sword back in its sheath (1 Chronicles 21:27).

Have mercy upon me, O God, according to Your loving kindness; according to the multitude of Your tender mercies, blot out my transgressions (Psalm 51:1).

Wake Up, Wake Up!

"Wake up, wake up!" my wife called. We had gone to sleep for the evening when my wife Jeanne heard a commotion outside our home in Haiti. I quickly dressed and went to the gate where some Haitian men were talking to our son Charles. "They're going to kill him," the Haitians said.

The explanation given was that a man in the area was stealing bicycles and selling them. They told me that at least 12 bicycles were stolen. Well over 100 men had surrounded the alleged thief. They were angry. Shouts were going up, "Kill him! Kill him!" In Haiti, retribution is often quick and violent. A captured thief is often beaten on the spot. If the crime is considered serious, he will be beaten to death.

What was I to do as a missionary, a pastor, a Christian? "Lord, help me," I prayed. I milled among the crowd talking calmly. I did not want to incite the men to mob action. "We are a civil people. Please don't hurt him. No, don't tear his clothes," I said. There was much noise, as everyone was talking at once.

"Lord, help me," I prayed.

Then, I further appealed to them. "Here in the dark of night we cannot think clearly. Let us wait until the sun comes up. We can talk better then," I said. "If tomorrow we believe him to be guilty, we can call the authorities; let them deal with him."

"Will you let him spend the night in my home?" I asked the crowd. "We would," some responded. "But when you are asleep, he will escape."

We have a small building at the mission that we call a *tikay* (little house). It is made of concrete with large iron-grate windows all around. The building is cool and is used for storing vegetables for our school kitchen. "Put the man in the tikay and lock the door," many shouted.

We agreed, and the man was locked in the tikay with our security man to watch him. I began feeling better. God was at work. I went back to bed, feeling that the man would be treated fairly in the morning. An hour later I was back in bed, the crowd returned with the thief's brother. He was asking for custody of his brother. I asked the crowd, "Shall I give this man to his brother?" They agreed. The man was set free and I was thankful.

Being a missionary in a place like Haiti requires the patience and wisdom of God. He is our helper in every situation.

If any of you lacks wisdom, let him ask of God, who gives to all liberally and without reproach, and it will be given to him (James 1:5).

The Great Journey

Famine broke out in the land of Canaan. Jacob with his children and their wives found refuge in the land of Egypt. The Israelites lived in Egypt for 400 years, first with great favor and finally under the harsh treatment of slavery.

Moses was used of God to lead Israel out of Egypt. They had come as a family; they went out as a great nation. Of that deliverance the children of Israel sang, "I will sing to the Lord, for He has triumphed gloriously! The horse and its rider He has thrown into the sea!" (Exodus 15:1).

The Call. After 40 years in the wilderness, Moses died. Now, God spoke to Joshua, "…go over this Jordan, you and all this people, to the land which I am giving to them—the children of Israel" (Joshua 1:2).

God works in each life to bring about His will. He arranges the circumstances; He speaks to us. The providence of God is at work to show us our task here on earth.

The Preparation. God prepares men for the task He chooses for us. Joshua was with Moses for forty years. Moses was his mentor. God only uses tested and proven men and women. God is at work today preparing us for a task that He has for us to do tomorrow.

*God only uses tested and
proven men and women.*

God knew the problems that Joshua would face in leading the people and establishing them in the Promised Land. The cities were fortified. The people were war-like. The Lord said to Joshua, "Never be discouraged."

The Vision. Joshua was not called to do every good thing. His task was to lead Israel into Canaan. We are to concentrate and stay focused on the work He has called us to do. The promise given to Joshua says, "...as I was with Moses, so I will be with you" (Joshua 1:5).

Our prayer is to hear His voice and His wisdom to obey.

...for the Lord your God will be with you wherever you go... (Joshua 1:9).

A New Generation

When New Missions first came to Haiti in 1983, our plan was to affect an entire area with the Gospel and then from this base to bring change to the country of Haiti. Real change begins by the preaching of the Gospel. The new birth results in a transformation of life. Then by providing a Christian education, the social, economic, and political life of a person changes.

The new birth results
in a transformation of life.

New Missions has 5700 students, with 700 in high school. Many of the students who are in high school started with us in kindergarten. Now that we have been working consistently on the Leogane Plain for so many years, we are seeing enormous change. This change is so great that it could be called a revolution.

When I was a boy growing up in Boston, there were horse and buggies in the streets. There was no TV, no jet planes, and surely no computers. I have seen great change. Now the pace of change has so quickened that we are taking quantum leaps. The social, economic, and political changes taking place are so broad and coming so fast that it has been described as a revolution.

To match these changes and bring correction to them, America needs a spiritual revolution. First Peter 2:9 says, "But you are a chosen generation...that you may proclaim the praises of Him who called you out of darkness into His marvelous light..."

Each generation needs to become this chosen generation. We are the light of the world, the salt of the earth and the yeast that leavens the entire loaf. I believe a spiritual revolution has also begun in America that will change the fabric of our nation. God will change the social, economic, and political makeup of America by a spiritual revolution. "The Gospel is the power of God unto salvation" (Romans 1:16).

We are in need of spiritual leaders who will rediscover who Jesus is and who will redefine the Gospel to speak to our generation, and who will preach Jesus with great courage, under the power of the Holy Spirit.

But you are a chosen generation, a royal priesthood, a holy nation, His own special people, that you may proclaim the praises of Him who called you out of darkness into His marvelous light... (1 Peter 2:9).

Only a Fool Says There Is No God

Can man by reason prove that God exists? The way to God is not through philosophical speculation.

Several arguments are put forth to prove God. The first is—there is a world; therefore, there must be a world maker. The second is—the universe is complex and full of design. Someone with intelligence must have planned it. The third is—from man's being. We are God-conscious creatures. We have a sense of right and wrong. Where did these ideas come from?

These arguments are meaningful to the believer. Yet, in fact, they do not conclusively prove that God exists. For me, God is self-evident. The Scriptures do not attempt to prove His existence. It simply says, "In the beginning God created the heavens and the earth" (Genesis 1:1).

There is only one way to come to know God. We do not seek Him out, but rather He has come to us. "God…who spoke in time past to the fathers by the prophets, has in these last days spoken to us by His Son…" (Hebrews 1:1, 2).

The Holy Spirit works to bring us to Christ. When we receive Jesus as our Savior, our spiritual eyes are opened, and we see the things of God. The only way to God is to believe. "…he who comes to God must believe that He is, and that He is a rewarder of those who diligently seek Him (Hebrews 11:6).

Faith does not look for proof. However, we have knowledge because "The Spirit Himself bears witness with our spirit that we are children of God" (Romans 8:16).

After we come to God, the first natural response is to worship Him. No other creature but man gives a conscious response to His Creator. Worship is the purest expression of faith. "Oh come, let us worship and bow down; let us kneel before the Lord our Maker. For He is our God, and we are the people of His pasture, and the sheep of His hand" (Psalms 95:6, 7).

"Lord, what do You want me to do?"

The second response is obedience. The question of the Jew has always been, "Lord, what do you want me to do?" Belief works into conduct. How are we to live? The first question of life is "Is there a God?" The second is "What is He like?" God is holy. The admonition of the Scriptures is to be holy even as He is holy. "...what does the Lord your God require of you, but to fear the Lord your God, to walk in all His ways and to love Him, to serve the Lord your God with all your heart and with all your soul..." (Deuteronomy 10:12).

The third response is service. To know Him is to love Him, and to love Him is to serve Him. God has sent us into the world. We are light, salt, and yeast. We light the world with the truth of God. We preserve the world by keeping it from falling into total sinfulness. We are to affect the world in all its aspects. We are to permeate every area of society with the truth of God in Jesus Christ. All of us have God-given abilities to be used in the service of our Lord.

The fool has said in his heart, "There is no God..." (Psalm 14:1).

God Is Love

Some Christians have emphasized the sovereignty of God and have made it the prime doctrine of the Christian faith. Surely, God is sovereign. He is Lord over all, and we worship Him as such. However, in the Scriptures, I believe the teaching that "God is love" is first and foremost. The essence of God's being is love.

The essence of God's being is love.

God loves with an everlasting love. From eternity past God knew us and loved us. And He will love us forever, all through the eternal future. I like what God said regarding Israel in Jeremiah 31:3, "…Yes, I have loved you with an everlasting love…" His love does not wane; it never diminishes. It is as sure as God Himself, for God not only loves. He is love.

God's love is unconditional. We never deserve, earn, or merit His love. It is bestowed upon us. Jacob was a scoundrel; yet, God said, "Jacob have I loved" (Romans 9:13). "…while we were still sinners, Christ died for us" (Romans 5:8). With all our sins, faults, and imperfections, He says, "I love you," and receives us as His children. "Behold what manner of love the Father has bestowed on us that we should be called children of God!" (1 John 3:1).

God's love is a tough love. As I write this, I think of David when he sinned with Bathsheba. God loved David before, during, and after

David's time with Bathsheba. God loved David; yet, He was just to bring correction into his life. "For whom the Lord loves He chastens, and scourges every son whom He receives" (Hebrews 12:6). That's tough love.

Here in Haiti, we have two grandsons with us, Nathan and Jeremie, and a granddaughter, Carita. They are two precious boys and a lovely girl who take much of the pain away of not being with family in the States. As I write these words, I ask myself, if one of them were disobedient, would I correct him or her? I want to see my grandchildren grow up to be good. I don't want to be a doting grandfather, but rather a good grandparent. I trust I have enough tough love to do the right thing. So it is with God. He wants us to grow up to be good. His love is a tough love.

And we have known and believed the love that God has for us. God is love, and he who abides in love abides in God, and God in him (1 John 4:16).

Spiritual Warfare: Intercession

Gospel work is spiritual work. Satan would hinder every advance of Christ if he could. He blinds the eyes of unbelievers so they will not see the truth that there is in Jesus Christ (2 Corinthians 4:4).

God breaks the powers of the enemy and gives liberty to the workers in the kingdom. Prayer brings the release of the Holy Spirit. Intercession is one of our most important tasks. Paul, in describing the armor of God in Ephesians 6, says, "Praying always."

Set time aside for intercessory prayer. I often awake during the night and spend two or three hours in Bible study and intercessory prayer. Alone with God, I can hear His voice, receive vision for the work, and intercede for victory.

Pray without ceasing. Learn to turn your thoughts toward God throughout the day. I enjoy good conversation with the missionaries, Haitians, and visitors. I laugh and banter with them. Yet just as soon as I am alone again, my thoughts turn heavenward. At that moment, right on the spot, intercession can be made. He is our victory! We need to be in constant communion.

Often we do not know how to pray.

Pray in the Spirit. Often we do not know how to pray. We do not always readily know the will of God. For example, if a senior Christian is terminally ill, do we pray "Lord, take him home peacefully" or do we pray "Lord, heal"? In Romans 8 Paul says that the Spirit helps us in our weakness. We can pray in the Spirit and the Spirit will make intercession for us. Paul says in verse 26 that the Spirit's intercession is made "with groanings which cannot be uttered."

The powers of the enemy must be broken over a life, a home and over nations. Some of our most important work is done through prayer.

> *...praying always with all prayer and supplication in the Spirit, being watchful to this end with all perseverance and supplication for all the saints...* (Ephesians 6:18).

To Know God

A ll of us need to be convinced in what we believe. We are thankful that we have the Scriptures. They convey the revelation of God to us. We are not left in darkness. God has spoken. He has shown Himself to us. Throughout our Christian life we should read, meditate upon, and study the Scriptures. It is by such discipline that our knowledge of God increases and stays focused.

Theology, simply put, is "God talk," or how we view God. Hopefully as we grow in our understanding of the Scriptures, our view of God becomes clearer; we might say "our theology changes." But remember that although our theology (how we view God) may change, God never changes. He is the "Unmovable Mover."

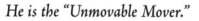

He is the "Unmovable Mover."

The Christian life is dynamic. We grow in grace, in faith, in service, and in understanding. The Christian ought not to have grass growing under his feet.

This is one of the reasons why I believe that the statement of faith we adopt for our churches should be true to the Scriptures and precise regarding the person and works of Jesus Christ.

Yet our statement of faith should embrace a wide variety of believers. The church should be a place where believers of different persuasions feel comfortable and can worship and work together.

By way of example, some believers hold to a pre-tribulation return of Jesus, others, a post-tribulation. Further, some believe there will be a millennial reign of Christ on the earth. Others believe that the millennial teachings in the Scripture represent the present time of the church triumphant.

In fact, Jesus never taught any of these views. He said, "I am coming back. Be ready." This is the message of the church. We are to preach that Christ died, resurrected, and is coming again.

We need to be true to the Scriptures, yet willing to accept people of various persuasions. Let us come together united in Jesus Christ; then, let us work together to bring the message of Christ to the world.

We ever rejoice, for we rejoice in Him who loves us and gave Himself for us.

Jesus Christ is the same yesterday, today, and forever (Hebrews 13:8).

A Satisfying Source

Cisterns are used for collecting and storing water. In areas of Palestine where there were no wells, people collected water from off their roofs. Often, rainwater flows downhill in tiny streams. This water too is directed to an underground cavern made of stone and mortar to be collected. Then in times when there is no rain, water is drawn for drinking, cooking, bathing, and animals.

The prophet Jeremiah likened God to a cistern. "For My people have committed two evils: They have forsaken Me, the fountain of living waters, and hewn themselves cisterns—broken cisterns that can hold no water" (Jeremiah 2:13).

Jesus visited Jerusalem during the Feast of Tabernacles. During the eight days of the feast, the people called to mind the miraculous blessings of Israel during their pilgrim journey. They recalled the manna given for food and the water that came from the rock.

Every morning for seven days, during the feast, water carried in a golden pitcher from the pool of Siloam was poured out in the Temple. On the eighth day, no water was poured out. On that day, Jesus stood and cried, "If anyone thirsts, let him come to Me and drink" (John 7:37). Here Jesus declared that He is the water of life.

Some people try to replace God
as the source of their life.

Some people try to replace God as the source of their life. They substitute God for religion, riches, education, and success. These are broken cisterns that cannot hold water. God alone can satisfy the longing and need of the human heart.

We have been blessed. At our mission in Haiti we have an artesian well. Water comes out of the ground from a shaft dug 185 feet deep. This water flows throughout our mission without a pump or gravity feed.

In simple terms, we have a lake underground with so much water in its cavity that it is under pressure. It is like a cistern. We draw from it continuously.

Some have asked, "Will it ever run dry?" My answer has been, "No. Never."

Whenever it rains on the mountains behind our mission, God is filling our cistern. Even so, the resources of God are everlasting. God wants and delights when we draw upon Him for our every need.

If anyone thirsts, let him come to Me and drink (John 7:37).

There are Three Things a Worker Must Do

Before the world was created, God knew you and chose you to show forth His glory. You were predestined to be a child of God. God also had a plan for your life, a work for you to do that would show His presence at work in the world.

Paul the Apostle put it this way: "…but I press on, that I may lay hold of that for which Christ Jesus has also laid hold of me… (Philippians 3:12). This involves life and service. We are to realize all that God has called us to be and then to realize the fulfillment of the work God wants to perform through us.

Life and service becomes intermingled to the point that you cannot distinguish one from the other. The work of Jesus cannot be separated from the person of Jesus. Noah and the building of the Ark have become synonymous. The work goes the way of the worker. When the worker is rich with life in the spirit, the work abounds.

Think and pray. Nothing happens without creative thoughts. As we pray and think, God works on our mind and shows us the work and how to accomplish it.

Be innovative. If a government, business, school, or church is unwilling to be innovative, it will miss a greater opportunity.

Work. Dreams are only fulfilled by hard work. My life has been full—full of dreams, innovation, and hard work. "I press on," Paul said. He put forth every effort to accomplish the work of God.

Not that I have already attained, or am already perfected; but I press on, that I may lay hold of that for which Christ Jesus has also laid hold of me (Philippians 3:12).

Dry Bones

Bleached, fragmented bones—their story has inspired believers for centuries. Ezekiel the prophet was asked of the Lord, "Can these bones live?"

"Can these bones live?"

What could appear more pathetic than a valley, in a desert, full of dry bones? In the Old Testament book of Ezekiel, chapter 37, speaks of Israel separated from her homeland and strewn among the nations. No more temple, priesthood, or prophet to speak to the people about the Word of God. Perhaps nothing could appear more hopeless.

Every bleak life situation can be seen in these circumstances. Dysfunctional families…the growing world drug problem…explosive AIDS . . the violation of human rights…and on an on. Haiti is a land riddled with fear, and superstition. The people cling to a culture that should have been outgrown years ago.

Is there no hope? Doesn't anyone care? Is there a word from heaven? God is not the God of the dead, but of the living. There is hope in God for every situation.

God commanded Ezekiel, "Speak to the bones." The bones came together, bone to bone. In my lifetime, Israel, as out of the tombs, has come back to their land. They are being connected bone to bone.

"Can these bones live?" Spiritual life will come to Israel. The prophet called upon the wind. The breath moved upon the bones—flesh, muscle, and skin came upon them. They stood up and became a mighty army.

Israel will be restored as the people of God. And what God is doing with Israel, He is doing in Haiti, and will do in your life. Nothing is beyond the concern and power of God.

In Haiti our children, young people, and adults are turning to the Lord. At the mission, 5700 are receiving a Christian education. Many of our graduates are finding employment. There is life at the mission. The wind of the Spirit is blowing. Deadness is turning to life.

I will put My Spirit in you, and you shall live...(Ezekiel 37:14).

The Inner Man

Conversion is not changing religions. It is not even living a good life. It is not formulating right doctrine. Conversion is coming into a right relationship with God the Father through Jesus Christ the Son. When a person believes in Jesus, the Holy Spirit brings life to the inner man. "…not by works of righteousness which we have done, but according to His mercy He saved us, by the washing of regeneration of renewing of the Holy Spirit" (Titus 3:5).

The inner man was dead due to trespasses and sin. The Holy Spirit comes to reside in the body and gives life to the soul. This we call the New Birth. "Therefore, if anyone is in Christ, he is a new creation; old things have passed away; behold, all things have become new" (2 Corinthians 5:17). Paul said we are in the Spirit if the Spirit of God dwells in us (Romans 8:9).

The Bible contrasts the inner man from the outer man. "The outer man perishes. The inner man is renewed day by day. We have this treasure in earthen vessels" (2 Corinthians 4:7, 16). The inner man will live forever, while the outer man is destined to die. In Romans 8:10, Paul says the body is dead because of sin. Man can destroy the body; he cannot destroy the soul.

The inner man affects the outer man.

The inner man affects the outer man. The body has many appetites. It needs food, clothing, shelter, and other amenities. All of these are necessary. Yet without restraint, they can go to the extreme. Man has a need for intimacy. However, if uncontrolled the need for intimacy could go on a rampage. Only the Holy Spirit can control the appetites of the body.

The Holy Spirit works on our mind. He causes us to be creative and to have the mind of Christ. The Holy Spirit touches our body. He energizes, comforts, encourages, and heals when we are ill. The Holy Spirit provides power for service and all of life's duties. Ever increasingly, the believer needs to depend on the Holy Spirit to work in and through the body to show God's glory in the world. Jesus said, "Out of your inner being shall flow rivers of living water."

What has happened to our souls, will happen to our bodies. The cross and redemption are for the whole man. Our bodies now grow old, weak, and die. One day that process will stop. We will receive new bodies. Jesus will transform our lowly bodies so that they will be like His glorious body (Philippians 3:21). "But if the Spirit of Him who raised Jesus from the dead dwells in you, He who raised Christ from the dead will also give life to your mortal bodies through His Spirit who dwells in you" (Romans 8:11). Redemption will be complete when our bodies are changed and all of creation is restored to its glorious original state.

"He who believes in Me, as the Scripture has said, out of his heart will flow of living water" (John 7:38).

We Have an Anchor

One of the themes of our mission since the day we arrived has been, "Haiti, hope in God."

In the Bible, the anchor is the symbol of hope. Hope speaks of the future. Hope is believing that good things are coming. We have hope for this life and for the life that is to come. "Every good gift and every perfect gift is from above, and comes down from the Father of Lights, with whom there is no variation or shadow of turning" (James 1:17). When we serve the Lord, we can expect good things to come to our lives.

The anchor is the symbol of hope.

An anchor is one of the necessary items on a well-outfitted boat. In fact, most boats have more than one anchor. A "lunch hook" is used for making short stops. And every good boat carries a "storm anchor." It is heavy and designed to hold in bad weather. In some situations, a boat will put out two anchors for added security. A wise sailor lets out as much line as he can when riding a storm. The longer the line, the more the anchor will hold.

Our anchor reaches into the Presence behind the veil. "This hope we have as an anchor of the soul, both sure and steadfast, and which enters the Presence behind the veil…" (Hebrews 6:19). Jesus entered the Holy of Holies in the heavenly temple. Our hope is not in some transient system or mortal person. It is in the eternal God.

Within the veil of the earthly temple was the mercy seat. Every year when the High Priest sprinkled the mercy seat with the blood of an innocent animal, Israel found pardon for sin and a renewed relationship with God. Today, the mercy seat of God is the cross. Jesus died and shed His blood so that we might be made right with God. The work of the cross is the only means of reconciliation. Our hope is in Jesus.

Our anchor will never fail. Regardless of the storms of life, we are safe in Christ.

This hope we have as an anchor of the soul, both sure and steadfast... (Hebrews 6:19).

Understanding Deception

Deception comes from many sources. For example, we know we can be *deceived by Satan*. We are not surprised when he uses his ploys against us. We need to remember that the devil is consistent: He never works for good. He is a liar and cannot tell the truth. For the believer who is walking in the light, it is easy to discern his tricks of deception. One favorite trick of his is to try to convince us that evil is good or that God does not have our best interests in mind. Satan entered the Garden of Eden as a serpent. That in itself was deception. He then worked cunningly to bring about the fall of Adam and Eve.

Sometimes we are *deceived by an enemy*. Our belief in the Gospel sets us in opposition with others. We believe that Jesus is the only Savior of the world. Our faith is in Jesus Christ and the work of the cross. Naturally, many people will not agree with us. Because of our stand for Jesus, some people may feign friendship and then work toward our failure. Haitians have an expression, "trompa," which means to trick or fool. They may trick you out of goods or money or trick you into doing them a favor. We should expect that some people will try to deceive us in this world.

Some people become *deceived by a friend*. That hurts! When we have put confidence in another person only to be betrayed, it's painful. Judas was part of the inner circle of trusted disciples, yet with a kiss he betrayed a friend. May our prayer be, "Lord help me to be true to my friends and may my friends be true to me."

———⊶⊶⊶———

*Haitians have an expression, "trompa,"
which means to trick or fool.*

———⊶⊶⊶———

There is a deception more devastating and more subtle than all of the above: *self-deception.* Sometimes we fool ourselves. "But be doers of the word, and not hearers only, deceiving yourselves" (James 1:22). We rationalize and provide reason to back up our wrong conduct. That is why reason is subject to revelation. We need to submit our minds and our thinking to the Word of God.

There is no deception worse than self-deception. It is self-imposed and often the hardest to be free from. We do not always have perfect logic or perception. Blind spots exist in the thinking process of all of us. Each day we need to pray and submit our lives to the Lord, asking the Holy Spirit to keep our hearts and minds.

Do not be deceived, my beloved brethren (James 1:16).

The Gardener

God is a creative Creator. Man is to be a worker with Him. When man was created, he was placed in a garden and given the responsibility to "tend and keep it" (Genesis 2:8, 15).

God loves order and beauty. In this fallen world, we, His new creatures, are to work. Work is a large part of our existence. What we do adds meaning and value to who we are. We find direction and guidance from the Lord to establish order out of the sometimes chaotic world.

My personality is such that I can't stand disorder. I have sat in churches that were unkempt and thought, "If I were responsible here...." Then I would make a mental list of remodeling and decorating ideas for the church. One time I stayed at a motel where the owner never seemed able to get organized. The caretaker hadn't cut the grass, the bushes needed trimming, and the trash—well—we won't talk about that.

Christians are the true idealists of the world. We know that sin is present in this world and things will never be perfect—until Jesus comes. We are not given to destruction, and confusion is painful to us. We work as the caretakers of God's garden. God is changing men and women by the power of His Spirit, who then are working to form a wholesome, peaceful environment for all to live in.

We work as the caretakers of God's garden.

The name George means "gardener." Next to my home in Haiti I have a small garden with coconut, orange, grapefruit, and banana trees. I also have tables upon which I grow a variety of vegetables, such as tomatoes, lettuce, and peppers. Having a garden brings me satisfaction. There is the convenience of having fresh fruits and vegetables when I want them, and there is also a satisfaction of seeing things grow. When I walk in the garden I sometimes feel akin to Adam: alone, walking with God.

My particular portion of the "spiritual" garden to keep is in Haiti. Haiti is full of confusion, superstition, fear, and oppression. It's a broken country. What a place for God to work.

May I ask you, "Where is your garden?" I encourage you to be faithful in doing the work of God.

Then he said to them, "The harvest truly is great, but the laborers are few; pray the Lord of the harvest to send out laborers into His harvest" (Luke 10:2).

One with Christ

One with Christ! This is our position. We are united with Christ in His death and resurrection. When Jesus died, we died. When He arose, we arose; now we are seated with Him at the right hand of the Father. This speaks of our mystical union with Christ. This union is symbolized in water baptism. When we were baptized, we went into a watery grave and came forth into newness of life (Romans 6:3-6).

Christ's victory is our victory. We are also one with Christ in His works.

Christ was a prophet. Jesus came to reveal the Father. He spoke as no man spoke (John 7:46). God, who at various times and in various ways spoke in time past to the fathers by the people, has in these last days spoken to us by His Son (Hebrews 1:1, 2).

Christ's victory is our victory.

The ministry of a prophet is one who speaks for God. In this world, we are to be His spokesmen. A pastor needs to wait upon God to receive a message. Then he stands alone, and without fear or favor, delivers the message.

We are all spokesmen for God. The life we live is a message but there can be no confusion. The message needs to be articulated. I have not come to Haiti only to do good works. I have come in the name of Jesus, and people need to know who He is and what He has done for us. I preach Christ crucified, risen, and coming again.

Jesus was also a priest. A priest offers sacrifice for sin. Jesus is our high priest who offered Himself—the Lamb of God, for the sins of the world. A priest speaks for the people. Many people are hurting. They need someone to bring them to God to experience His love and grace. Haiti hurts! Millions are lacking essential food, clothing, or shelter. They often ask, *Does anyone care?* Yes, God cares and He has sent us to Haiti to be priests to the people—to bind up their wounds and bring healing in the name of Jesus.

Christ the King. Jesus, in coming to earth, laid aside His glory to identify with us in our humanity (Philippians 2:6-8). While upon the earth, He demonstrated His Kingship. He was Lord over disease, demons and death.

When He fed the 5,000 with fish and a few loaves of bread, He was saying, "In My Kingdom, there will be no hunger." When He healed the sick, He was saying, "In My Kingdom, there will be no sickness." When He forgave sin, He was saying, "In My Kingdom, there will be no sin," and when He cast out demons, He declared, "In My Kingdom, there will be no devil."

We share in the Lordship of Christ. Revelation 1:6 says we are priests and Kings unto God. Upon arriving in Haiti, I found confusion, fear, superstition, and oppression. We immediately set about establishing order and good government throughout the mission.

While upon the earth, Jesus was a servant King. He washed feet and upon His entry into Jerusalem, He rode on a donkey—what a paradox. Upon the cross they wrote, "King of the Jews." We share with Christ in His Kingship and when we serve, we rule.

The future will be glorious. When Jesus comes again He will come to rule as sovereign Lord. And we will rule with Him.

> *Therefore, if there is any consolation in Christ, if any comfort of love,*
> *if any fellowship of the Spirit, if any affection and mercy, fulfill my*
> *joy by being like-minded, having the same love, being of one accord,*
> *of one mind* (Philippians 2:1, 2).

In God We Trust

W e're moving back to India," a friend exclaimed. The man and his wife were our good friends. They came to the United States to attend a university and then stayed for several years to work. "Why are you going back to India?" I asked. "America has so much to offer," my friend began. There was much about America they liked. But, now their children were beginning to grow up and they didn't want them to imbibe too much of the American culture. "In India, we are much more conservative. The home life is strong and we are not influenced by negative television. I don't want my children to grow up in America," he explained.

America has drifted. Crime, drugs, abortion, family breakdown, and the flaunting of homosexuality have filled our society.

Whenever people lose faith in a personal God, they tend to live for self and make a god of materialism and pleasure.

Can America turn around? Can the moral downward spiral be reversed? I have had some friends say, "There is no hope for America; it is on an irreversible catastrophic course." I have prayed much about this. "Lord, is there hope for America?" I have asked. I see a lot of Christians who are determined to live for Jesus and bring a change to America.

The foundation of any nation is its spiritual beliefs. America is strong economically, militarily, and technologically. The problem of America is spiritual. The secularists have preached that there is no personal God and have advocated a free style of life. This has led to a moral breakdown of the nation. Clearly, America was built upon the belief of a transcendent God who created the universe and is involved in the lives of individuals and nations. God has revealed Himself. Jesus is the full disclosure of who God is. The Son is the Savior of the world. This is the foundation upon which America was built and which made her great.

Whenever people lose faith in a personal God, they tend to live for self and make a god of materialism and pleasure. Living for self can only lead to destruction, first of the individual and then of the nation. We need something bigger then ourselves to live for. Only God can give meaning to life and give purpose for living. We need something bigger then ourselves to consume our thoughts, plans, and energies.

First Peter 2:9 says that we are "a chosen generation." I believe that this generation of believers has been chosen to rebuild the foundation of faith in God. By living according to the revelation of God's Word, we will bring America back—back to where it belongs: A nation living with its "trust in God."

Some trust in chariots and some in horses, but we will remember the name of the Lord our God (Psalm 20:7).

The Kiss of Heaven

*F*or the gifts and the calling of God are irrevocable" (Romans 11:29). The gifts and the calling have been given to us and will never be retracted.

The work of the Holy Spirit is myriad. We are gifted and graced by the Holy Spirit. He leads, empowers, and gives us wisdom and knowledge. The Comforter has come.

One of the outstanding works of the Holy Spirit is to anoint. The anointing comes with the call, and the gifts cause them to function efficiently. The anointing enables. It is the touch of the Divine. It is the kiss of heaven. The anointing makes the difference between the mundane and the magnificent.

When I was a pastor in the States, every Sunday I graded my message as far as its effectiveness to communicate God's Word to the hearts of the people in the congregation. I graded myself from one to five. One meant that I blew it; five, I was at my best. Needless to say, every time I preached, I strove to know the anointing and to preach a full five.

The anointing makes the difference between the mundane and the magnificent.

You cannot declare the anointing for yourself, nor can you give it to another. We are reminded of Jesus' words, "You did not choose me, but I chose you and appointed you that you should go and bear fruit, and that your fruit should remain..." (John 15:16). God alone can give a ministry to a man or a woman. God called Moses, Isaiah, Gideon, and Samuel. Elijah did not call Elisha. He even tried to discourage Elisha. God places men and women in places of leadership. God sent me to Haiti and placed an anointing on the mission. I didn't ask for it. Now, I pray that one day the anointing will come upon someone else to continue the work that I've started. I can pray, but I cannot decide who the person will be. That is the work of the Holy Spirit.

God often chooses the seemingly incompetent to do His work so that God may receive the glory. Moses said, "I cannot speak," Isaiah said, "I'm sinful." Gideon said, "I'm a nobody." Samson is a good example of God choosing ordinary people to do extraordinary things. Under the anointing, the Philistines trembled. Without the anointing he was "like other men." "...not many wise according to the flesh, not many mighty, not many noble are called" (1Corinthians 1:26).

The call and gifts need to remain. The anointing is enjoyed so long as we are true to Jesus. We live in relation to God the Father through Jesus Christ. Sterile gifts come about by a lack of obedience. So long as we walk in dependent humility to the Son of God, we will enjoy the richness of His anointing. Under the anointing, God will use us mightily to show Himself to the world.

Now He who establishes us with you in Christ and has anointed us
is God, who also has sealed us and given us the Spirit in our hearts
as a guarantee (2 Corinthians 1:21, 22).

A Miracle Roof

My heart was pounding! Finally, after many months of prayer and planning, the building to house the Royal Caribbean Institute was under construction. The site had been prepared months in advance. But weeks of construction on the road leading into our mission compound from the highway had delayed the work on the building.

The building we were putting up is directly across from the existing high school classrooms. The new building was to mirror the existing building. It's the same design, with the same windows and doors and, of course, the same red roof tiles that are on all the buildings at the high school campus.

The windows and doors for the building were ordered, as the floor was poured and the blocks put in place. A beautiful ceramic tile was selected for the floor. I measured the roof and figured out that we needed 470 of the six-foot tiles to cover the roof.

God delights to give us miracles…

Bouchard is the only company in Haiti that sells these tiles, which were imported from the Dominican Republic. Naturally, I went to them to order the roofing material. Over the years I have purchased thousands of tiles from them and have a good relationship with the owner. I went to his office. "Raymond," I said, "I need 470 tiles for a building I am putting up." "Sorry," he said, "I don't have any and will not be importing any more. The Haitian government is placing too heavy a tax on the tiles, and I would never be able to sell them to the Haitians at the new price."

Putting different roofing material on the new building would destroy the decor and look foolish, I thought. "Lord, what shall I do?" For days I prayed, pondering different options that I had. But none of them seemed right. "God, there must be a solution. Help," I prayed.

That Sunday evening we had a staff meeting and a time of prayer with our mission team. "Pray with me" I asked, and I shared my dilemma with them. After the meeting I stepped out the back door of the lounge where we were meeting and looked up at our storage building. God said to me, "There is your roof!" The storage building had the exact same roof that is on the high school building. Immediately I measured the building. It was 95 feet long, and the building we were putting up was 91 feet long, so there would be more than enough of what we needed.

The next day we began removing the tiles. Within a week the tiles were off, in excellent condition, and a metal roof was put on the storage building. This experience reminded me that God is the answer to our every need. Never despair. Pray. God delights to give us miracles, even the miracle of a red roof.

Unless the Lord builds the house, they labor in vain who build it...
(Psalm 127:1)

Run with the Vision

The following are three essential ingredients of a worker for God: *First, the worker for God has strong convictions.* We need to know what we believe. Yes, there are areas of uncertainty where we are ever looking for better understanding, such as the nature of the Second Coming of Jesus Christ. And the debate over eternal security rages in the church. But, there are areas where we take a strong stand.

We believe in God. We believe that Jesus is the Son of God and the Savior of the world. We believe that God has spoken and His Words are written in a book that we call the Bible. These truths are the basis of our lives, and for them we are willing to give our lives.

*Without clear direction, God's people flounder,
go in circles, and live in confusion.*

Secondly, we are growing spiritually. The Christian life is one of progress. We are ever learning to be conformed into the image of Jesus. In this life we will never arrive. We are always growing. To stop growing is to begin to regress. The last thing we would want is for the Lord to say we are "lukewarm." D. L. Moody said, "My life is a leaky vessel; I ever need to be refilled." Growth is natural in all of life, and it is essential to our spiritual well-being (Hebrews 5:12-14).

Thirdly, we are men and women of vision. We are not required to do every good thing, but we are required to do what God asks of us.

Vision comes from God. We receive the vision from Him and then pass it on to others.

In the Old Testament when there was no prophet through whom God could speak, the Bible said, "And the word of the Lord was rare in those days; there was no widespread revelation" (1 Samuel 3:1). We need men and women with whom God is speaking today to give clear direction. Proverbs 29:18 says, "Where there is no revelation, the people cast off restraint…" What to do. How to do it. When to do it. All of this comes from the Lord. Without clear direction, God's people flounder, go in circles, and live in confusion.

The vision is ongoing. Everyday a leader looks to God for guidance. As Israel had the cloud by day and the pillar of fire at night, even so God gives guidance for His people to do His work.

Receive the vision from God, then run with the vision.

Trust in the Lord with all your heart and lean not on your own understanding; in all your ways acknowledge Him, and He shall direct your paths (Proverbs 3:5, 6).

Job: A World Example

*T*he book of Job gives us important insights into the spiritual realm; it shows us the nature of God and the character of Satan.

The devil is a thief. He took all of Job's possessions, his cattle, his house, and his children. He smote Job with boils over his entire body, and he wanted to kill him. Job's three friends asked what sins he had committed to deserve such suffering. His wife told him to "curse God and die," (Job 2:9). Job's reputation was gone, and the devil was after his soul.

In the book of Job we see that God knows everything about us, and His watchful eye is ever with us. God is concerned for His people. Here we see the nature of God at its best. The devil complained, "Have you not made a hedge around him, his household and around all that he has on every side? You have blessed the work of his hands, and his possessions have increased in the land" (Job 1:10).

The devil wants to put you down
and keep you down; Jesus wants to lift
you up and keep you up.

Satan cannot touch us without God's permission. God is our sword, shield, buckler and strong tower; we are "kept by the power of God" (1 Peter 1:5).

God has a hedge of protection around us, but it is our responsibility to maintain the hedge. Through right living, prayer, study of the Scriptures, fellowship with believers, and being active in Christian service, we maintain the hedge.

Remember, the devil wants to put you down and keep you down; Jesus wants to lift you up and keep you up.

In the end Job was fully restored, his possessions doubled, children were given to him, and he was esteemed by his friends. Job is a world example of how God cares for His own.

...who are kept by the power of God through faith for salvation ready to be revealed in the last time (1 Peter 1:5).

God Speaks and Delivers

God has made Himself known. In the Old Testament, God spoke through the prophets. God could not remain silent and still be God. For the Creator not to communicate with His creatures would be counter to who He is. God loves us and has made Himself known to us.

Moses is an excellent example of God speaking. After killing an Egyptian, Moses fled to Mideon. There he married Zipporah, and cared for the flock of Jethro, his father-in-law. Then it happened. One day as Moses was leading the flock in the desert, he saw a bush burning. He watched, expecting it to be consumed. When he came close to the bush, a voice spoke to him. "Take your sandals off your feet, for the place where you stand is holy ground" (Exodus 3:5).

Israel had been in Egypt for 430 years. Slavery had oppressed them. God appeared to be nowhere in sight. We often cannot understand our circumstances. Sickness may afflict us. Our finances may be lacking. Never despair. We need to look beyond the immediate and hear from God who speaks and delivers.

For the Creator not to communicate with His creatures would be counter to who He is.

God spoke to Moses and sent him back to Egypt. And with a mighty hand, God brought Israel out of Egypt and led them to the Promised Land. God still speaks and works on our behalf today.

In these last days God has spoken to us through His Son. Prophets are of God. However, when God wanted to speak clearly and directly to us, He sent Jesus. Jesus came to show us the Father. He said, "Therefore, whatever I speak, just as the Father has told Me, so I speak" (John 12:50).

Moses was given the Ten Commandments for Israel to know how God wanted them to live. They were to be a covenant people, living apart for God. Jesus, too, has taught us how we are to live. He taught that we are to love God and love our neighbor. The law of love is the new command that Jesus has given us. God loves us. We, in turn, are to love Him and to make love the basis of our relationship with everyone else.

Jesus is our Deliverer. He delivers us from the devil and from sin that would destroy us. Jesus died for our sins. Now there is not the external keeping of the law, but internal salvation from sin. Sin no longer has power over us. We are free from condemnation. Moses delivered Israel from slavery in Egypt and the oppression of Pharaoh. Jesus delivers us from the power of sin. He gives us new life and the power to live for Him by the indwelling of the Holy Spirit.

My sheep hear My voice, and I know them, and they follow me (John 10:27).

Purpose and Vision

Often people who visit our mission ask, "What is the purpose of New Missions? "Why are you working in Haiti?" I am always glad to share our vision.

Haiti has a long history of mismanagement. Leaders have often used their political office for their own financial gain. The consequences have been a high illiteracy rate, a lack of development, 80% unemployment, poverty, and disease.

We do not believe that Haiti will change overnight and become like America.

First and foremost we have come to Haiti because God has sent us here. We are on a mission for the Lord.

Second: We are working to raise up a new generation of people in Haiti. The cycle of corruption, poverty, ignorance, and superstition needs to come to an end. A new generation needs to be established.

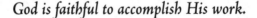

God is faithful to accomplish His work.

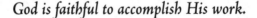

Third: Real change takes place on the inside. This is where we begin and upon what we build. When a person believes in the Lord Jesus, the Holy Spirit comes to live within creating a new person. At that time, old things pass away, and all things become new (2 Corinthians 5:17). Our first responsibility in Haiti is to bring people to faith in Jesus Christ.

Fourth: Then change begins to come to the other areas of life. Education provides intellectual and social change. Opportunities for employment open up and economic change takes place. And this new generation, I believe, will one day affect the political climate of the country.

We at New Missions are concentrating our time, finances, and spiritual energy here on the Leogane Plain. Thousands of children and young people are coming to know Jesus as Savior and receiving a quality education. We are raising up a new generation in Haiti.

God is faithful to accomplish His work. Our task is to stay focused and close to Him.

But seek first the kingdom of God and His righteousness, and all these things will be added to you (Matthew 6:33).

Foundation for Living

*T*he basis of a life, a family, a business or a nation is its beliefs. America has been built upon the Judeo-Christian faith. Our belief in God gives us meaning to life as well as the will and purpose to live.

We believe that God existed before anything existed. He made all things and is supreme over all creation. This God is personal. He knows and cares for us. He has the hairs of our head numbered and provides our daily bread.

Jesus is the rock upon which we build our lives.

We believe that God spoke in times past through the prophets. He has drawn especially close to us by sending His Son Jesus Christ into the world. Jesus came to die for our sins and by the work of the cross, reconcile us to the Father.

These are our basic beliefs and upon them we base our lives. Jesus is the rock upon which we build our lives. The Christian lives before God. In Him we live and move and have our being.

Secularism is the death of America. It brings about the disintegration of lives and thereby our American way of life. The secularist says, "There is nothing beyond what can be known through the senses." When a person does not have a belief system, when there is not something all-encompassing that affects his life; he is then forced to live for himself.

The result is greed, self-fulfillment, and often, pleasure. The problem with much of America is the lack of faith in a personal God. The consequences of such an attitude is evident: broken homes, children born out of wedlock, drugs, crime and eventually disillusionment. Paul, the apostle, summed it up many years ago: "If the dead do not rise, 'Let us eat and drink, for tomorrow we die!'" (1 Corinthians 15:32).

We as believers have a responsibility to bring the message of the Gospel to our society. *We need to rediscover* who Jesus is. It is the greatest story ever told. *We need to redefine the Gospel.* Every generation is different. Jesus is the same, yet the situation of our generation is unique. The message of Jesus must be applied to the 21st century. *We need a fresh anointing.* Every Christian is called to prayer, a life of discipline and a personal walk with God. We have a work to do. I believe that with God's help it will be accomplished.

Therefore thus says the Lord God: "Behold, I lay in Zion a stone for a foundation, a tried stone, a precious cornerstone, a sure foundation; whoever believes will not act hastily..." (Isaiah 28:16).

Loyalty: Is It a Lost Virtue?

I like the word "loyalty," but it is not found in the Bible. The closest synonym is the word "faithful."

In Matthew 25, Jesus spoke at length of His return to earth. He told the story of a man who went on a long journey and left the responsibility of his affairs in the hands of others.

These responsibilities were spoken of in terms of talents. One was given five, another two, and another one. They were to invest what they had and increase it. The first two doubled their talents but the third went and hid his. The one who had five and the second who had two were commended, "Well done, good and faithful servant; you were faithful over a few things I will make you ruler over many things." The person who hid his talent was reprimanded. "You wicked and lazy servant." He was cast out into outer darkness.

I wonder—are we losing our sense of loyalty. There was a time when individuals got a job with a company and worked there for the rest of their lives. Now the turnover in places of employment is every three to five years. Companies downsize and employees looking for advancement change jobs. People are encouraged to become knowledgeable, make themselves sellable, and go where they can earn the most money. Today there is little commitment on the part of the employer or on the part of the employee.

Has this attitude of "faithful to self" pervaded our society? Has it crept into our spiritual and domestic life as well? "I go to church to get a fluffy feeling," one Christian told me. "I go to be blessed and if I don't get it in one church I'll go to another," she quickly exclaimed. This attitude is difficult for me. Maybe I'm old-fashioned, but I always believed that God led people into a church, and that they went to be a blessing and stayed forever, or at least until God led them elsewhere. Now, church hopping is as common as sampling the chocolates at a Fanny Farmer's candy store.

Think of marriage. Forty percent of first-time marriages end in divorce. When I was a child, I had never heard of divorce. Then I began to hear of non-believers getting divorced. Now it's full blown in the church. I believe that divorce is a tragedy. Pastors need to reach out to people going through such a wrenching experience. The divorcee needs to know of God's love and forgiveness and be nurtured into the fellowship of the church.

But what about our young people? What is our message to them? Is there any validity to the wedding vows? Aren't we to warn of the hurts and pitfalls of divorce? Do we teach loyalty, faithfulness, and commitment to our youth? There needs to be a turnaround, and it must begin with this next generation of young people.

Revelation 2:10 has always spoken strongly to me. "Be faithful until death and I will give you a crown of life." We are called to be faithful in the face of death. It also speaks to me of daily living for Jesus over a long lifetime.

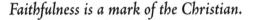

Faithfulness is a mark of the Christian.

Faithfulness is a mark of the Christian. This trait needs to be nurtured. One of the great characteristics of God is that He is faithful. Psalm 119:90 says, "Your faithfulness endures to all generations..." Let us allow Him to work His faithfulness into our lives.

Be faithful until death and I will give you the crown of life (Revelation 2:10).

Are We Equal?

The French Revolution forced social change in the country of France. Out of the revolution came three words, "Liberte, Egalite, Fraternite," which translate "Liberty, Equality, and Brotherhood." Haiti was a French colony, so these words have become part of the Haitian constitution. In the United States, Thomas Jefferson wrote the Declaration of Independence. He said, "We hold these truths to be self-evident, that all men are created equal."

Are we equal? And if so, in what way? Surely, not all people are equal economically. Each of us has a different income and we are free to use it at our own discretion. Some people would like to use the graduated tax structure to more equally distribute wealth. Instead, I believe Christians collectively and individually should keep more of what they have earned to help those who are less fortunate.

Socially, we all come from different settings. I happen to be the son of Italian immigrants. My parents left Italy because at the time, Italy was poor. The Italians went to America looking for a better life. I am thankful for my heritage. I didn't have as much as many others, but America did give me the opportunity to go to Bible college and graduate school.

Biologically, we have all inherited different things from our parents. We differ as far as height, weight, looks, innate gifts, and intelligence.

Are we equal before the law? The Haitian judicial system is weak. The judges are underpaid, the courthouses are in shambles, and the prisons are deplorable. Justice in Haiti is often determined by your status in society and the amount of money you have. In America, the judicial system is not perfect, but it is many times better. The symbol of justice is a woman with a balance in her hand and a blindfold over her eyes. The problem in America is that not everyone can afford to hire the best lawyers. Some people who have no money are given a public defender who works on a limited budget. Only those who have amassed a fortune can afford the best lawyers.

The only place where true equality exists is with God.

The only place where true equality exists is with God. We all have equal access and are treated the same by God. "...God shows no partiality. But in every nation whoever fears Him and works righteousness is accepted by Him" (Acts 10:34, 35).

One of the images of God in the Scriptures is that of a judge. The devil is often likened to the prosecutor. He is the accuser. He knows what we did wrong and is quick to point it out. The law requires that the sinner be punished by death. Satan says, "I know what he has done. I was there when he did it."

Thank God we have a good lawyer to plead our case. Jesus is our advocate. He quickly steps forward to say, "Yes, he is guilty, but I died on the cross for his sin. I paid the penalty for his wrongdoing. Father, pardon him on my behalf." Because of the cross, the Father is able to justify and remain just. Christ died for the sins of the whole world. All may come and receive forgiveness. We have equal access and equal treatment before God. "Red and yellow, black and white, we are equal in His sight."

Then Peter opened his mouth and said, "In truth I perceive that God shows no partiality. But in every nation whoever fears Him and works righteousness is accepted by Him" (Acts 10:34, 35).

Hope in the Midst of Horror

Jeanne and I love Haiti, yet we lament over its present condition. When Christopher Columbus landed in Haiti, he found a virtual paradise. When the French controlled the colony, it was the envy of the European nations. Haiti was then called "The Pearl of the Antilles." It was the richest of all the colonies. It produced more wealth than all the thirteen American colonies combined. Today, Haiti is in shambles. The government is inept, the economy is devastated, there is little infrastructure, and the people are left poor and hungry. Jeanne and I grieve over the conditions here in Haiti.

Jerusalem was a beautiful, proud city. The temple had been the focus of Israel's spiritual life. Now, it all lay in ruin. The city of Jerusalem was reduced to rubble and the temple had been destroyed. The Babylonian hordes ravaged the city and took the young men and women off into captivity.

Jeremiah the prophet, overlooking the devastation, laments. He writes, "…how like a widow is she, who was great among the nations!" (Lamentations 1:1). "Her adversaries have become the master… because of the multitude of her transgressions. Her children have gone into captivity before the enemy" (Lamentations 1:5). In the midst of tragedy, Jeremiah saw a day of triumph for Israel. "Through the Lord's mercies, we are not consumed, because His compassions fail not. They are new every morning; great is Your faithfulness. 'The Lord is my portion,' says my soul, 'Therefore I hope in Him!'" (Lamentations 3:23, 24).

God is a dreamer. He had a dream for Israel and sent Nehemiah and Ezra to return from captivity to rebuild the temple and walls of

Jerusalem. We are never left in despair; regardless of the circumstances, we look to God. He is the source of our hope. God is at work in Haiti. He has sent us to start a restoration of the country.

---

*We are never left in despair; regardless
of the circumstances, we look to God.
He is the source of our hope.*

When we came to Haiti, we had nothing. We lived in tents, slept on the ground, and washed in the stream. Today, we have ten elementary schools, a full high school, and a college. In total we have 5700 students in school. This is God's doing.

I see America on a new surge of spiritual life. From time to time, I return to the States to preach in churches. This gives me a wonderful opportunity to visit different parts of the country and preach in many different congregations.

For the longest time I felt that the spiritual life of America was in despair. Now I have experienced a new excitement; people are coming to faith in Christ and the pastors are enjoying the work of the Lord. America, I believe, is turning around. Prophets in the land are speaking God's Word, and a true turning is taking place.

On a larger scale, I also see hope for the world. Resistance to the Gospel exists in many places, especially in the Islamic nations. Today, however, there are faithful missionaries working in those difficult places. Some of the nations seem impossible to reach. But I am reminded that God is the God of the impossible. He tore down the walls of communism in Russia and Europe in what seemed like a day. Thus, He is able to remove obstacles and hindrances to the Gospel of Jesus Christ. God's plan is not only for America or countries such as Haiti, but for the whole world. "For the earth shall be full of the knowledge of the Lord as the waters cover the sea" (Isaiah 11:9). God has a dream for the salvation of the whole earth.

Each of us needs to be a Nehemiah or an Ezra, looking to God for wisdom and strength, then uniting heart and mind to return to the rubble of the world, and finally in the name of Jesus begin to rebuild.

Why are you cast down, O my soul? And why are you disquieted within me? Hope in God, for I shall yet praise Him for the help of His countenance (Psalm 42:5).

Discovering
God's Special Purpose

"Why was I born? What is the purpose of my existence here on earth?" A look at the life of Samson will help us to answer these questions.

Over the 400 years that cover the book of Judges, Israel was on a spiritual roller coaster. God would send a deliverer to Israel; they would live in victory. Then all too often, Israel would begin to serve other gods, and again an enemy would come to oppress the nation.

In Judges 15, God raised up Samson to deliver Israel from the Philistines. Three things were notable in the life of Samson. *Before Samson was born, he was selected by God.* Samson was not yet conceived and God chose him. An angel appeared to Samson's mother and said, "Behold, you shall conceive and bear a son…" (Judges 13:7).

God's hand is upon each and every person.

Before any of us were born, God knew us and chose us to know, love, and serve Him through Christ Jesus. God's hand is upon each and every person. Some people are selected to be preachers or Bible teachers; others are selected to be business people, medical people, computer personnel—the list is endless. In whatever situation God places us, we are to be a light and make Jesus known to those around us. Each of us has a sphere of influence for the Lord. We are all called to minister for the Lord. Each of us is important and in our own way we speak the Word of God. Jesus said, "Let your light so shine before men, that they may see your good works and glorify your Father in heaven" (Matthew 5:16).

Samson had a purpose for his life. "… and he shall begin to deliver Israel out of the hand of the Philistines" (Judges 13:5). Most people in the Scriptures who were selected by God had a single purpose. Noah built an ark, Moses delivered Israel from Egypt, and John the Baptist was the forerunner of Christ. Even Jesus had a singular purpose for His life. As a missionary, I'm not called to do every good thing. God has given me a special task in a particular country.

Some people are forever trying to discover what it is that God wants them to do. The Scriptures encourage us: whatever your hand finds to do, do it with all your heart. Most often, the thing God wants you to do is right in front of you.

Samson's parents were told what type of a man Samson was to be. He was not to cut his hair or to eat or drink anything that came from a grapevine. This was called a Nazarite vow. Samson was to be separated unto God from the time of his conception in the womb.

Samson soon discovered what kind of man God chose him to be; he was then able to fulfill the purpose of God for his life.

We are never good in our own sight; our goodness comes from God. Our strength is not innate; the Lord is the strength of our lives. It is the Holy Spirit living within us who controls our lives, gives us strength, and makes us the men and women God wants us to be.

When we received Jesus as our Savior, he became our Lord. "I have been crucified with Christ; it is no longer I who live, but Christ who lives in me…" (Galatians 2:20).

For we are His workmanship, created in Christ Jesus for good works, which God prepared beforehand that we should walk in them (Ephesians 2:10).

God Speaks

How do we come to know God? Is it necessary that we search for Him? Some religious people have sought Him for a lifetime only to be disappointed. In reality, however, we do not look for God. He comes to us.

We do not look for God. He comes to us.

Yes, we can know God and have a personal relationship with Him. God is looking to have an intimate relationship with each of us. There are four ways by which God speaks.

First, *God speaks through nature.* We can look at creation and know that God is there. The Psalmist said, "The heavens declare the glory of God and the firmament shows His handiwork" (Psalm 19:1). What we see of God in creation is that He is our Creator. We see an intelligent, powerful being.

Second, *God speaks to us through Jesus.* Jesus is a special way that we hear from God. In times past, God spoke to the fathers by the prophets, but in these last days He speaks to us by His Son (Hebrews 1:1, 2). In Jesus, we learn of God's love, compassion, and salvation. We hear a clearer, more distinct message in the life of Jesus; God says "I know you and I care about you."

Third, *God has spoken and what He has said has been written in a book.* That is the meaning of the word Bible. It is the book from God.

Today, it is the clear voice of God. We need to read, understand, and heed the messages of the Bible.

Fourth, *God speaks to us personally.* God has not gone off on a long journey so that when we call Him all we hear is silence. God is involved in our lives. He wants us to talk to Him and He wants to talk to us. Often in prayer I have heard God speak to my heart and say, "I love you."

We were visiting Haiti on a regular basis before we started our mission in 1983. For three years we looked at a piece of property. One day, while walking across the land, I asked, "God, what do you want me to do about this land?" Clearly, God spoke to me and said, "George, go with it." Upon the basis of those words we bought the land, came to Haiti, and founded New Missions.

God speaks. Listen. And you too will hear His voice.

Behold, I stand at the door and knock. If anyone hears My voice and opens the door, I will come in to him and dine with him, and he with Me (Revelation 3:20).

God's Blessing

Blessing comes from God. God is a good God and His desires and plans for us are always good. With God there is no "variation or shadow of turning."

Each of us enjoys a measure of God's blessing. Some have their feet wet with the blessing of God, others are up to their ankles, some to their waist, while others are swimming in the blessing of God. We don't always know why God loves and blesses us. Some of it, I believe, is due to our response to Him. Come to God. Give Him your life—the blessings will come.

"Give me five dollars," a beggar once said, "and God will bless you." I told that person, "I'm already blessed. I don't have to give you five dollars to receive the blessing of God."

We cannot earn the blessing of God. It is not tit for tat. I do not serve God for what I will get from Him. I serve God because it is in my heart, it is my duty. I give not to receive but to bless others.

Blessing is conditional. God expects us to live right. Be faithful. We are to serve the Lord to the best of our ability. God wanted Israel to enjoy His blessings. Yet in 2 Chronicles 7:14, He said, "If My people who are called by My name will humble themselves, and pray and seek My face, and turn from their wicked ways, then…" That was conditional. "I will hear from heaven, and will forgive their sin and heal their land."

Blessings are to be shared. God loves to give. He gave His only Son to die for us. He is the ultimate example. When God called Abraham, He said that He would bless Abraham and that Abraham would be a blessing to all people (Genesis 12). We know that Jesus was of the lineage of Abraham. Jesus is the seed of Abraham, and it is God in Christ who is blessing the whole world.

Selfishness is inconsistent with the Christian life.

What we receive, whether it be spiritual, material or informational, it is not for ourselves alone; it must be shared. Selfishness is inconsistent with the Christian life. "...it is more blessed to give than to receive" (Acts 20:35).

Blessed be the God and Father of our Lord Jesus Christ, who has blessed us with every spiritual blessing in the heavenly places in Christ... (Ephesians 1:3).

Stretching

We all enjoy a good stretch. Some of the exercises that we do, such as bending over and touching our toes, are designed especially to stretch the tendons in our body. Athletes and dancers stretch all the time. We've all seen a cat wake up from a nap and stretch.

Most of us want the security and comfort of the familiar. God often puts us in the unknown and in places where responsibilities are upon us. These ultimately work to make us a more mature, well-rounded person.

First, *God wants to stretch our understanding of Him.* Many of us have a small God. Some think of Him as an old man sitting on a throne in the sky. Some think He's a monk in a monastery. Yes, our knowledge of God is limited to what we see in creation and what is written of Him in the Scriptures. Yet, even Scripture tells us that God is beyond what words can describe. "For My thoughts are not your thoughts, nor are your ways My ways," declares the Lord in Isaiah 55:8,9. "For as the heavens are higher than the earth, so are My ways higher than your ways, and My thoughts than your thoughts." God is awesome.

Second, *God stretches us in the work we do for Him.* He often starts us out doing simple tasks. One of the first tasks God gave me was to conduct an evangelistic meeting in a city park. My responsibilities have grown immensely since then. A Haitian woman who does our bookkeeping started out working in our mission kitchen. "Some day," I used to tell her, "you'll have an important, good-paying job." She is now our mission bookkeeper. Another young man started by washing our vehicles. Today he is the manager of our food warehouse, school kitchen, and our grounds workers. Today's responsibilities are often God's preparation for tomorrow's enlarged service.

Third, *God wants to stretch our person*. From the day we were conceived we've been growing physically, intellectually, and spiritually. My formal education was in the area of the Bible, theology, and philosophy. I've grown to enjoy reading economics, political, and social science. As of late, I've been learning the computer, and of all things, I am learning Spanish. God is stretching me as a person, I believe, for further areas of Christian service.

In Isaiah the 54th chapter, the prophet spoke of Israel's future glory. Verses 2 and 3 say, "Enlarge the place of your tent, and let them stretch out the curtains of your dwellings; do not spare; lengthen your cords, and strengthen your stakes. For you shall expand to the right and to the left."

God is at work in our lives, developing us into the person He wants us to be.

God's stretching process is often painful, but God is at work in our lives, developing us into the person He wants us to be.

Now to Him who is able to do exceedingly abundantly above all that we ask or think, according to the power that works in us, to Him be glory in the church by Christ Jesus to all generations, forever and ever. Amen (Ephesians 3:20).

What Is God Like?

"What is God like?" I am often asked. Quickly, I think of all the "omnis:" omnipresent, omniscient, omnipotent. These are helpful to understand the nature of God. Yet they are limited. Words cannot fully describe who God is. And any description only ends up being a limitation. For me it is best to say, "God is God and He is awesome." However, what we do say about God must be limited to the revelation of God in nature and in the Scriptures.

God is beyond definition. The only way to know Him is to experience Him. Back in the 70s I did a fair amount of ministry on Cape Cod, Massachusetts. We rented halls in each of the major towns on the Cape to hold a Gospel Rally. Cape Cod is a wonderful place. Much has been written about its beauty. But all the words that could be said or written could never take the place of you personally spending time on Cape Cod.

For us to know God we must experience Him. It is for this reason that Jesus has come. In Him we see the Father and through Him our relationship is established with the Father.

The attributes of God that excite me the most are His moral attributes. There is a long list of these. God is holy, just, merciful, faithful, patient, constant, forgiving, and loving.

Atheists have a hard time dealing with love. If men evolved over millions of years from some primordial plasma, then at what point did man begin to love and where did it come from? The atheist has no answer.

We as Christians know that these virtues come from God. The wonderful thing is that when we receive Jesus as our Savior, then the

Holy Spirit comes to dwell within us and He begins to work the nature of God into our character. God teaches us patience. The love of God is shed abroad in our hearts. These are the fruits of the Holy Spirit. We not only know God as an objective being, we experience Him subjectively and receive His nature into our being.

We not only know God as an objective being, we experience Him subjectively and receive His nature into our being.

Do we know God perfectly? No. Now we see through a glass darkly. Yet we are promised that one day we will see Him face to face. Then we will know even as we are known. God has made Himself known. He is making Himself known in the lives of His people. And the day is coming when there will be a full disclosure. The heavens will part and we will see God in all of His beauty.

For the Lord Most High is awesome; He is a great King over all the earth (Psalm 47:2).

Comfort in the Rain of Life

None of us are immune from hurts and problems. "Man is born to trouble, as the sparks fly upward" (Job 5:7).

All my life I have believed God for good things. And good things have come to me. I enjoy a good family and many friends. Good health has been mine. The ministry I'm involved in gives me much pleasure. Yet, none of us are exempt from problems, heartache, and stress. When I was 16 years old my father was killed in an automobile accident. When I was 21, my mother, at the age of 58, died of an enlarged heart due to asthma. We live in a fallen world; both good and evil exist. The rain falls upon the just and the unjust, and thank God the sun shines upon us all.

Haiti is a hurting land. The people struggle for survival. Many of the basic ingredients for a decent life are missing, such as sufficient food, good drinking water, affordable health care, and the opportunity for employment.

All ministry is based upon relationship.

One of the ministries of the Lord is to comfort. The Holy Spirit is called the Comforter. Second Corinthians 1:3 says, "Blessed be the God and Father of our Lord Jesus Christ, the Father of mercies and the God of all comfort..." All ministry is based upon relationship. On a one-to-one basis we need to encourage people. We need to come to know their hurts and comfort them. Recently, I watched a report on a ministry in Brooklyn, New York, called Metro Ministries. They bus 18,000 children and young people to Sunday School every week. When asked the reason for the success of this ministry, Bill Wilson, the founder, said, "We care about these kids; every week each one of them is visited in their home. Our ministry is based on relationship."

The same comfort that the Lord extends to us needs to be given to those we meet. The people we minister to in Haiti are like anyone in the world in that they have needs and hurts. For us to truly minister to them, we need to know them and care for them. As missionaries, we do not just preach to people. We need to understand their lives, their concerns and needs, and in the Spirit of Christ comfort them. God said in the Old Testament, "Comfort, yes, comfort My people!" (Isaiah 40:1). Even the ministry of Jesus was "to heal the brokenhearted" (Luke 4:18).

Blessed be the God and Father of our Lord Jesus Christ, the Father of mercies and God of all comfort, who comforts us in all our tribulation, that we may be able to comfort those who are in any trouble, with the comfort with which we ourselves are comforted by God (2 Corinthians 1:3, 4).

I Am Mind-Boggled

An important theme of the Bible is how God's goodness is extended to all men through Jesus Christ. There is no message like the message of God's love shown to us at the Cross. "...while we were yet sinners Christ died for us" (Romans 5:8).

There is nothing more spectacular to contemplate than the Incarnation. Our minds "boggle" to think that the eternal God became a man: He lived and walked among us. It is even more mind-boggling to think that Jesus, the Son of God, so loved us that He died, at the hands of men, on a cruel Roman cross.

It boggled everyone's minds when He came back to life from the dead. The Roman soldiers were mind-boggled as well as the woman who went to the tomb to anoint Him. Even the Apostles were boggled by the Resurrection. Thomas declared, "Unless I see in His hands the print of the nails, and put my finger into the print of the nails, and put my hand into His side, I will not believe (John 20:25).

It is mind-boggling to think of the Second Coming of Jesus to this earth. "How and when will it happen?" men ask. We are told that He will return with all of the saints and angels. What an ushering in! The whole earth will shake. The King of kings and Lord of lords will come, riding upon a white horse, with the shout of all the redeemed. Mind-boggling—yes! True—Yes!

My mind is happily boggled thinking of the prospects of the next life that is to come.

When Jesus comes, we will be changed. Now we struggle, living in this earthly body. But then we will have a new body: no sickness, hunger, injustice or sorrow—mind-boggling—yes! My mind is happily boggled thinking of the prospects of the next life that is to come. "But as it is written:'Eye has not seen, nor ear heard, nor have entered into the heart of man the things which God has prepared for those who love Him'" (1 Corinthians 2:9).

The mind of the world, on the other hand, is troubled. It is bogged down with doubt, criticism, self-deception, and the painful emptiness of insecurity. Wanting to live by fact, they never come to faith. Without a clear knowledge of God they despair in uncertainty. They cry, "I don't know."

It is hard to be in darkness. It causes you to live for the moment, to live for self and to extract every ounce of pleasure possible out of this life, for what else is there?

My mind is boggled because I do not now fully understand. But I am full of excitement because the future is open-ended. I am going to be with God and will enjoy Him forever. Even as I write this, the Spirit leaps within me. He says, "Be happy, for the good things that God has for His children will shortly come to pass." As a Christian, I am not bogged down by guilt, shame, fear or unbelief. Rather, my mind is happily boggled because the goodness of God is over-whelming in its extent and prospect.

But as for me, I would seek God, and to God I would commit my cause-who does great things, and unsearchable, marvelous things without number (Job 5:8, 9).

To Please God

To live in such a way that God is pleased with us should be the desire of every believer. We have a relationship with God that is as real as any human relationship here on earth. Every relationship must be established and then maintained. Relationships can lose their luster or they can become richer over time.

There are some essentials in maintaining a good relationship with our spiritual Father. First, *we enter into a relationship with the Lord by faith.* "He that comes to God must believe that He is." The Bible admonishes us to believe and be saved. The faith for our salvation must be fixed in the person and work of Jesus Christ. We enter into relationships with the Father when we receive Jesus as our Savior.

Faith is also ours for life. We are encouraged to trust God for every life situation. Problems do come. When they come, we look to God for help. He is our strength, guide, wisdom, and security.

When we speak of the faith, we also refer to the teaching of Scripture. There are some basic teachings in the Scriptures that Christians consider part of the faith. We agree on the Fatherhood of God, the person of Jesus, and the work of the Holy Spirit. We keep our beliefs true to the teaching of God's Word. The first thing *we need to do to live pleasing to God is to walk in faith.*

Second, *we need to walk in harmony.* Soldiers march in step. Together they form a formidable force. The last thing a soldier wants to do is break rank and run. Together we are strong. Christians do not have to form one massive world organization to be one. Jesus makes us one. Paul wrote, "For by one Spirit are we all baptized into one body..." (1 Corinthians 12:13).

———— ⟨∞⟩ ————

Together we are strong.

———— ⟨∞⟩ ————

In Jesus there are no denominational barriers. It is wonderful when diverse believers come together, set aside their differences, and worship and work together.

Harmony also speaks of how we walk together. A group can be physically together and yet be out of step in their inner feelings toward each other. The mark of the church has always been "look how they love one another." The Holy Spirit unites heart and mind as well as body.

Another important ingredient to pleasing God is to walk right. The Christian is different from other people of the world. Certainly we do not consider ourselves above or better than others. We do not look different. We have many of the same needs and desires as everyone else. For example, we enjoy family life and we play sports and love recreation. However, we are different. God knows everything about us and directs our lives. He occupies the thought life of a believer. We live to please Him; in this we are different. The Scriptures hold an authority over our lives and dictate how we are to live. We are keenly aware that good conduct pleases God."…just as you received from us how you ought to walk and to please God …(1 Thessalonians 4:1).

Therefore we make it our aim, whether present or absent, to be well pleasing to Him (2 Corinthians 5:9).

In the Garden

In my garden in Haiti I have green pepper plants. Whenever we need peppers I pick a few of the better, bigger ones. There were a few small peppers that I kept waiting to grow. Instead, they turned red and dried up in the warm Haitian sun. For the longest time, there they were, at the top of the plant, bright red, yet undeveloped and shriveled up.

One day the Lord spoke to me through those peppers. They were on the plant, yet they had lost their usefulness. "Help me, Lord," I prayed, "to not be like these peppers, in the Lord, yet lacking vitality." Then I made a list of essentials needed to remain vibrant for the Lord.

Know what you believe. What you believe is important. I believe that God exists. I believe that Jesus is the Son of God and that His death upon the cross is the only means of salvation. I believe that the person of the Holy Spirit is with us, and it is He who leads and energizes the believer. By faith in Jesus we enter into a personal relationship with the Father. This is the essence of Christianity.

Many people have no faith in God and cannot begin to know about life in the Spirit. Some Christians have allowed their faith to come into question. They are no longer sure about what they believe. That is a sure way to become dry on the vine.

Worship. Our mission team in Haiti comes together regularly to worship and share God's Word. Also, whenever I attend one of our Haitian churches, I endeavor to enter into the presence of God and worship Him. Of all God's creatures, we alone can consciously, with heart and mind, recognize our Creator and worship Him. Worship is essential for our spirits to be lifted and refreshed.

Pray. The best prayer for me is spontaneous. Wherever I am or whatever I am doing, I turn to the Lord and pray. Once, at a Christmas party, I suddenly felt the need to pray. I closed my eyes and prayed for a few minutes. The presence of the Lord came upon me. I looked up and saw our hostess staring at me with a puzzled look, probably wondering, "What is he doing?"

It is necessary to set designated times to pray. But for me, praying on the run works best. Paul's words, "Pray without ceasing," encourage me.

Be Generous. We need to be responsible people. We need to care for our families and make preparation for their anticipated future needs. Unexpected emergencies might arise and money should be set aside for these. But we should also have a ministry of care for others. To live only for self can rot our bones, but a generous spirit is like healthy marrow. Jesus knew this. He said, "It is more blessed to give than to receive" (Acts 20:35).

Ultimately, Christianity is a life lived.

Live Right. Disobedience or conscious sin is a scourge. Nothing will dry the life of God from us faster than sin. Nothing! Ultimately, Christianity is a life lived. Our lives are to be shining testimonies to the grace of God at work in us.

These five principles will keep the vitality we have in the Lord alive. Not only do I have peppers in my garden, but a variety of vegetables are growing wonderfully. My prayer is, "Lord, make me like Joseph, 'a fruitful bough...His branches ran over the wall'" (Genesis 49:22).

I am the vine, and you are the branches. He who abides in Me, and I in him, bears much fruit; for without Me you can do nothing (John 15:5).

The Reluctant Missionary

_T_he word of the Lord came to Jonah. He was to go to Ninevah and call the city to repentance. Jonah was a prophet in Israel. Ninevah was the capital of the Assyrian Empire. The Assyrians repeatedly invaded Israel. Time and again the best men and women in Israel were marched off to slavery in Assyria. Because of it great animosity existed between Israel and Assyria. Jonah, no doubt, did not want the Assyrians to hear the Word of God. Therefore he fled to Joppa and boarded a ship to Tarshish. He was a prophet running away from God.

A severe storm arose and it was determined that Jonah was the cause. The men threw him into the sea where God had prepared a great fish to swallow him. What a place for a man of God—in the belly of a great fish!

There are three things that I want us to learn from the story of Jonah. _First, God deals with his prophet._ We as humans often write off people who have failed. That is not God's nature. Jonah prayed in the belly of the fish. God heard his prayers, restored him, and told the fish to vomit Jonah up on the shore. The Bible says, "Now the word of the Lord came to Jonah a second time." What a lesson of God's love for His people. Rest assured that God has forgiveness for you, regardless of your disobedience. God will restore you and fill your life again with His love, joy and peace.

The second thing I want to talk about is judgment. Severe, physical judgment had come in the Old Testament: the flood of Noah and the fire and brimstone on the cities of Sodom and Gomorrah. The Scriptures tell us of terrible days that will come upon the earth in the last days. Judgment will also come to every person when we stand before God to give an account of what we have done in this life. However, judgment can come today. When Adam sinned he was separated from God. We often want to make light of our sins. Remember, Adam only sinned once and it separated him from God.

In this life, it is intended that we be filled with the Holy Spirit to the degree that He overflows our lives. This is a life of bliss. When we keep our hearts right, we have fellowship with God and good things fill our lives. When we are disobedient, we allow Satan to rob us of our joy. That for me is the worst form of judgment. To have less than all of God's fullness in our lives is an immediate and heart-rending judgment.

What a place for a man of God—
in the belly of a great fish!

The last thing I want to speak about is the goodness of God. Jonah preached and Ninevah repented, then God changed His mind regarding sending judgment to the city. Jonah was not pleased. He wanted judgment to fall. He was angry. "... Ah, Lord, was not this what I said when I was still in my country? Therefore I fled previously to Tarshish; for I know that You are a gracious and merciful God, slow to anger and abundant in lovingkindness, One who relents from doing harm" (Jonah 4:2).

Jonah went to a high hill to sulk. The sun was hot and the heat caused exhaustion. God made a plant to grow to cover Jonah's head. Then a worm ate at the root of the plant and a hot east wind blew upon it and the plant died. Jonah felt sorry for the plant.

God spoke to Jonah. "You have had pity on the plant for which you have not labored, nor made it grow...And should I not pity Ninevah, that great city, in which are more than one hundred and twenty thousand persons...?" Here we see a picture of the heart of

God. Without a doubt, He has a heart for Israel, but He also has a heart for all the other nations of the world. Jesus died on the cross for the sins of all people. God is no respecter of persons. He so loved the world...

> ...(God is) *not willing that any should perish, but that all should come to repentance* (2 Peter 3:9).

Trophies for God

Athletes are often given trophies—perhaps a statue, cup or medal for their outstanding achievements. Actors are given Oscars as awards; business people are typically honored with plaques. Some people have collected so many awards that they have a trophy room.

God, too, collects trophies. However, they are not gold medallions or physical objects. Rather, the trophies of God are His people. Job certainly was a trophy of God. "Then the Lord said to Satan 'Have you considered my servant Job, that there is none like him on earth, a blameless and upright man, one who fears God and shuns evil?'" (Job 1:8).

God changes our lives and holds us up as His trophies to show that He is alive and at work in this world.

The believer, while in this world, is not perfect. At the new birth we receive a new nature. Old things have passed away, behold all things have become new (2 Corinthians 5:17). We have a new nature, yet we retain our old nature. The believer is a composite. We are capable of serving God and doing good. And we are capable of carnal activities. God has a plan for us in eternity. He also has a plan for us in this world. The natural bent of man is to sin. God's plan is to work in us causing us to live for Him. This is a supernatural work. By

His love and grace God works in our lives so that the things we used to do, we don't do anymore. God changes our lives and holds us up as His trophies showing that He is alive and at work in this world.

The Gospel is the power of God unto salvation (Romans 1:16). We are saved by the work of the cross and yet salvation will not be complete until our bodies are raised from the grave, changed and united with our spirits. I am saved, yet I am being saved. God is at work in me and He saves me everyday. This is a process. I need Him constantly in my life. He keeps me, helps me, and changes me. As such, the believer is the trophy of God showing His power in the life of the believer. God's grace is sufficient for all things. There is nothing too hard for the Lord. When conduct is changed for the better, bad habits are broken, or a marriage relation continues to grow, it is because of God. He is at work. When you face a trial, whether it be financial, relational, physical or emotional, and you work your way through it—that is God. His grace is sufficient. As Paul said, "...But where sin abounded, grace abounded much more..." (Romans 5:20). When someone walks faithfully with God for a lifetime it is not because of his innate goodness or ability to endure. No! It is because of God. At the end of our lives, after much trial, persecution, hardship and labor, God receives the glory. He works in us making us what He wants us to be. We are God's trophies in this world. And in the world to come we will be a spectacle all through eternity showing the love and power of God and His grace that has come to us through Jesus Christ. We will shine brighter than the stars and forever say, "But by the grace of God I am what I am..." (1 Corinthians 15:10).

But thanks be to God, who gives us the victory through our Lord Jesus Christ (1 Corinthians 15:57).

Where Are We Going?

*I*am often asked where New Missions is going. What I am really being asked about is my vision for New Missions. First of all, vision originates with God. How could I begin to propose what is best for Haiti or for the ministry of New Missions? It is God who has a plan—for the whole world, for Haiti, and for New Missions. For New Missions, God reveals His plan slowly, one step at a time. Ultimately, the redeemed will be with the Lord both rejoicing and working in His eternal kingdom.

When we arrived in Haiti in 1983, very few children were attending school. Now, in our area, virtually all the children are in school. In 2000 we will have a total enrollment of 5700 students; of that, 700 are in high school.

God gives the vision, shows how the vision will come about, and tells when the vision will be fulfilled.

Enormous change is taking place. When we started working in the Leogane area, few people had a college education. Today, the Saint Croix Hospital, which operates in Leogane, transports technical and clerical people from the capital city of Port-au-Prince to work at their hospital.

Now Leogane has a college, the Royal Caribbean Institute School of Theology. This school will play a vital role in the years to come, providing pastors, teachers, administrators and business people for the area. We have the potential of changing the entire area spiritually, economically, and perhaps even politically.

When I was a child, God had His hand on me and worked my childhood experiences to prepare me for my life's work in Haiti. As a youth of 19, God came into my life. In my own bedroom I had a burning bush experience. He told me who I was to be, where I was to go and what I was to do. He never asked me; He still doesn't. God moved in and took over. He invaded my life! Paul said he was "apprehended." He was a chosen vessel to the Jews and then to the Gentiles. Like Paul, I am His to obey, and God sent me to Haiti and to the Dominican Republic.

For the past few years, we have been bringing New Missions to a greater level of maturity. Yes, we have been growing, by about 500 students a year, but our concentration was primarily on training leaders. We were also in great need of buildings. Recently several churches and school buildings have been built, helping us to prepare for more serious growth. Evangelistic efforts will be enlarged and much prayer will take place for new churches to be planted. A strong base has been built in Haiti from which to expand. Considering what has been accomplished in the past, starting with nothing, who knows what God will do in the years ahead. Within Haiti, we also have our Jerusalem, Judea, Samaria and the ends of the world.

God gives vision, then He shows how the vision will come about, and lastly, He tells when the vision will be fulfilled.

I will instruct you and teach you in the way you should go; I will guide you with My eye (Psalm 32:8).

The Man with the Plan

We often fail because we forget that the work of the ministry is God's work. God is on a mission. He invites us to share in the work. "We are laborers together with God." God calls us. He sends us. And when we go, *He shows us what we are to do.* We are only responsible for what He gives us to do. How liberating!

Noah was told to build an ark, Nehemiah to rebuild the walls of Jerusalem, Joshua to take the city of Jericho, Paul the Apostle to preach to the Gentile nations. Today, apostles are sent to plant churches. Others are sent to the nations of the earth.

It so happened that Jeanne and I were sent to Haiti. In Haiti we were given specific instructions. We were sent to the Leogane Plain. This is a coastal plain about 6 miles wide and 12 miles long, 20 miles from the capital city of Port-au-Prince.

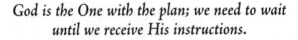

God is the One with the plan; we need to wait until we receive His instructions.

The next town down the highway from where we are located is the town of Grand Goave. God has not sent me there—at least not yet. I know that if I went there to start a church, the Lord would say, "George, what are you doing? I have not sent you to Grand Goave." Also, the finances that He provides to run our mission would be spent in the new work, and soon the mission would be hurting. I do not have to do anything—except what God asks me to do.

After telling us what to do, *God tells us how to proceed.* He gives us perception. He tells us how to accomplish the work He has sent us to do. Noah was given the dimensions of the ark, the design, the type of wood. God didn't only tell Joshua to take Jericho—He also told him how to take the city. In silence, all the people marched around the city once each day for six days. On the seventh day, they marched around seven times, turned, faced the walls of the city and began to shout. Hebrews 11:30 says that "By faith the walls of Jericho fell."

In the natural, these were foolish instructions, but can you imagine Joshua at the end of the day marveling at the great work God had done? God is the One with the plan; we need to wait until we receive instructions from Him.

Thirdly, God has perfect timing. *He will tell you when to do the work.* God often speaks to His servants regarding things that are to be accomplished months, even years, from now. Patience is necessary for working in the Kingdom. Be anxious for nothing. In the natural we want to accomplish everything today. God has a time schedule, as in the coming of Jesus to earth; it was in the fullness of time—and God has a time set when Jesus will come again.

For us to get out of step is often to miss God's best. Remember, God can accomplish more in a day than we could do in a lifetime.

Never fear that God won't speak to you. He is looking for people to send into the harvest. Wait upon the Lord. He will show you what to do, how to accomplish it, and when to begin.

The counsel of the Lord stands forever, the plans of His heart to all generations (Psalm 33:11).

Chosen

Divine selection has always fascinated me. I often ask, "God, why did You choose me?" First, I was chosen to receive eternal life, and then, God put me in the ministry. Why? I am convinced that Israel was chosen arbitrarily. God is God and He can do whatever He wants. Can the clay say to the potter, "Why have you made me this way?" I don't believe the Jewish people were more spiritual, intelligent or submissive. On the contrary, they were obstinate and often rebellious. But according to Divine selection they were chosen. I am convinced that in Jesus Christ, the whole world is elected to salvation. God doesn't want anyone to be lost. He loves the whole world. His desire is that everyone will hear of His Son and decide to receive eternal life. God has chosen the whole world—elected them to salvation—but we are free; we have a will and can reject God's call upon our lives.

The call of God came to my life: "Follow me!"
The only thing I did was to say, "Yes."

Here I am a missionary in Haiti. How did I get here? I was born in Boston, the son of immigrant Italians. The Italian young men of Boston didn't typically go to the mission field. They went to the universities, and then into businesses. What happened to me? The call of God came to my life—"Follow me!" Jesus said. I was not of a special pedigree. The only thing I did was to say, "Yes." I love the story of Jacob in Genesis. Jacob and Esau were twins, but Esau was born first, and as the elder son, was to become the head of the family. Esau was a hunter. One day after returning from the woods, he was hungry and felt he would die. Jacob had made a succulent meal of lentils, and Esau asked for some. "Give me your birthright and you can eat all you want." Esau replied, "If I don't eat, I'll die, and then of what use will the birth right be to me?" Therefore, he sold his birthright for a bowl of lentils. Later, when he realized what he had done, he hated his brother. When Issac their father was old and could not see, he knew death was near. Issac wanted to bless his older son, Esau, and told him to prepare a meal of venison for him. Rachel, Jacob's mother, over-heard the conversation and prepared a meal for Jacob to give to his father so he could receive the blessing in the place of Esau. While Esau was in the field hunting, Jacob put on hairy clothes and pre-tended to be Esau. When he appeared before his father with the meal, Issac asked, "Who are you?" "I am Esau," he answered. "Tell me," Issac asked, "are you really Esau?" "Yes," he said. Issac then proceeded to bless Jacob, bestowing upon him the family riches and making him the head of the family above his brother. Jacob was a scoundrel and a liar, as his name implies, and yet in Romans 9:13, it says of God, "Jacob have I loved and Esau have I hated." Why? How could God love a deceiver and a liar? The difference was that Jacob loved the things of God. Jacob was forever saying "Yes" to God. Esau, however, disre-garded the things of God. Why has God chosen me? There is noth-ing special about me. I am not a genius. I am not some holy, holy person. The only thing I can think of is that I keep saying, "Yes! Yes! Yes, God." Even as God blessed Jacob, He pours His blessings into my life. I know that what God has done for me, He will do for you. Begin saying "yes," and keep saying "yes" to Him every day.

...He chose us in Him before the foundation of the world...
(Ephesians 1:4).

Growing in the Knowledge of God

Buffeted by Satan, Paul prayed for the removal of a "thorn" in his flesh, only to hear the Lord say, "My grace is sufficient for you, for My strength is made perfect in weakness" (2 Corinthians 12:9).

God calls us to do a work for Him. That work is important, and for its accomplishment He gives us His gifts. In the midst of the work, God wants to make Himself known to us. Haiti is a wonderful place to serve God, but it is not heaven. It is not free of its problems. Every day we are called to lay down our lives. Living out of our culture is painful. We are in real-life situations. Yet it is here that I come to know God in ever deepening dimensions. Life is the crucible for God to form our character. God is at work and He uses every situation that we face to show us His love, His strength, and His grace.

---

*Life is the crucible for God
to form our character.*

In the midst of the work, problems arise; there are irritants and conflicts. We would like to be free of them, but our spiritual senses tell us, "that's life here on planet earth."

We come to know God by the experience of salvation. We come to know Him better through the Scriptures and we continue to know Him as He shows Himself daily by working in our lives. There is much to learn about God. So much that it will take all eternity for us to know Him perfectly.

"Don't forget," I said one time, "School begins again the Monday after Easter." These were my words to the students at the Royal Caribbean Institute School of Theology. Students in Haiti often do not come to school for several days after a holiday and sometimes miss up to a full week. I wanted our students to be different. I had dreams of them being truly a "new generation."

The Monday after Easter, seven students showed up in the Business School and none in the Education School, not even the teachers! Maybe it was my pride, but I was devastated. My deep feelings were "I've done so much to provide for this school, the teachers, building, books—my whole heart has been put into this school." I was deeply involved with the school. Now disappointment set in. And worst of all, I shared my feelings with the students after they all were in attendance. Where could I turn but to the Lord. Slowly, healing came! God poured in His love—for me, and for me to love my students. Strength to resume my leadership was given and, of course, God is faithful to provide grace for every occasion.

When we see a good marriage we need to glorify God and see how His grace has worked in the union. When we see a man or woman being steadfast in duty throughout life—we see God at work pouring out His love, strength and grace. Paul, the seasoned soldier said, "But by the grace of God I am what I am... (1 Corinthians 15:10).

And we know that all things work together for good to those who love God, to those who are called according to His purpose (Romans 8:28).

No Wood, No Fire

Only the Holy Spirit can put a flame in our hearts. The more we allow Him to reign in our lives, the greater will be the glow. It is He, the Holy Spirit, who adds passion to our lives. Enthusiasm can come from the natural man. But natural enthusiasm can run out of steam, especially in the face of adversity, difficulty, or hard work. The Holy Spirit, on the other hand, gives a zest for life that turns the most mundane task into joyous excitement.

Too often people think of passion solely in terms of sex, and they have difficulty talking of passion as strong feelings, enthusiasm, and zest for living.

The Holy Spirit gives a zest for life that turns the most mundane task into joyous excitement.

Passion can go astray. Both the Scriptures and life are replete with examples of casualties—men and women who had runaway passion. King David is a prime example. Misdirected passion will destroy. This is why we must always be careful what we fuel our passions with. The wrong fuel will cause strange fire that can only destroy a life. A controlled fire is productive. An uncontrolled fire is destructive.

Some people seemingly never develop a passion. One well-known college professor said, "I ask my students what they'll do after school and too many respond, 'I don't know.'"

Most of us like our drinks either hot or cold, but never tepid. We respect people who are hot or cold but not lukewarm. Mediocrity is never appreciated. If we can't get an "A" for achievement, we can at least get an "A" for effort.

Paul was a man of passion. "Woe is me if I don't preach the Gospel," he said. All of this comes from the Father, Son and Holy Spirit. God is full of passion. He loves the whole world! Jesus said, "I have come to do your will, O God." The Holy Spirit is the life of the church and is at work in the world making Jesus known to everyone.

A college student was among a group that came to work in Haiti. He asked me what I read. "The Bible," I said. "Yes, but what else?" he inquired. I had to admit I enjoy reading political science, social science, and some economics. But the passion of my life is the work God has given me to do in Haiti and the Dominican Republic.

It is possible to have a passion and lose it. Like a natural fire that constantly needs more wood to keep the fire burning, we need to receive from the Holy Spirit on a daily basis. "Where there is no wood, the fire goes out..." (Proverbs 26:20). Remain focused, stay close to the Lord, and the fire will burn strong all the days of your life. I do not believe we need to go whimpering out of this world at the end of life. Rather, beginning in childhood and lasting through old age, we can be filled with passion for life and Christian service. And then we can go home to be with the Lord like a rocket on its way to Mars.

...not lagging in diligence, fervent in spirit, serving the Lord (Romans 12:11).

How to Succeed

The Christian does not measure success in terms of popularity, money or numbers. Success is being all that God wants us to be.

In my life some things have proven invaluable in realizing my dreams. *First, be convinced.* It's hard to sell a product in which you have no confidence. With all my heart I believe that God has shown Himself in three persons: Father, Son, and Holy Spirit. I believe that the work of the cross is the only means of salvation. Jesus Christ is the bedrock of my life. And the Scriptures have an authority over my life. Paul said, "…for I know whom I have believed…" (2 Timothy 1:12).

Success is being all that God wants us to be.

Second, we need to know where we are going. We must have a sense of direction. What does God require of me? God always works the circumstances of my life to bring me where He wants me to be. As I did the thing at hand with all my heart and mind, God brought me to the next place for my life. "The steps of a good man are ordered by the Lord" (Psalm 37:23).

Next, stay focused. It is easy to get side-tracked. Most people who are successful sought to do just one thing, and they continued to seek to do it better. Some people feel that they are obligated to do every good thing. I am not responsible for the whole world; I am only responsible to do what God has given me to do. Coca-Cola has one goal: sell more Coke! Paul said, "I press toward the goal..." (Philippians 3:14).

Fourth, use adversity as a stepping stone. "Yet man is born to trouble, as the sparks fly upward" (Job 5:7). We cannot eliminate conflict, stress, problems or adversity from our lives. For a leader, they come with the job. Some people allow problems to overwhelm and discourage them. Bill Gates, the founder of Microsoft, would be considered a highly successful businessman. Does he have problems? Whew! I'm glad I don't have his problems. Yet, Microsoft, I believe, will continue to grow and experience great achievements. Use your problems as stepping stones to bring you to new heights.

The secret of success is to do what is right. We are not perfect, we are human; yet God's grace enables us to live lives pleasing to Him. I have seen people who were not Christians and did what was right and got blessed. And I have seen believers who did what was wrong and suffer severe consequences.

Sanctification means "to be set apart." The man whose heart is right is the man who will succeed.

Only be strong and very courageous, that you may observe to do according to all the law which Moses My servant commanded you; do not turn from it to the right hand or to the left, that you may prosper wherever you go (Joshua 1:7).

Samson:
Tragedy and Triumph

*F*rom before his conception in the womb, Samson was set apart to God by a Nazarite vow. While his mother carried Samson in the womb, she was not to eat anything unclean or to drink wine. The angel of the Lord had instructed Samson's parents that he was never to cut his hair or drink anything that came from grapes. God's plan for Samson was to use him to deliver Israel from the oppression of the Philistines. The Bible records that Samson grew and the Lord blessed Him. "And the Spirit of the Lord began to move upon him…" (Judges 13:25).

Samson is a symbol of the Spirit-filled believer. Note something about "life in the Spirit." First, the Holy Spirit comes into our lives at the new birth. Jesus said, "That which is born of the flesh is flesh, and that which is born of the Spirit is spirit" (John 3:6). Regeneration takes place by the Holy Spirit. After this, we are to grow in life in the Spirit. This is then a life-long experience.

Samson's power came by the
Holy Spirit upon his life.

There is often confusion regarding the Holy Spirit. Some people think of Him as a "force" or the power of God. He can seem to be ethereal. Rather, the Scriptures clearly speak of Him as being a Person. He is as much a Person as the Father or the Son. And He is equal with them. When we receive Jesus as our Savior, the Person of the Holy Spirit comes to dwell within us. "…your body is the temple of the Holy Spirit…" (1 Corinthians 6:19).

The Holy Spirit who comes into our lives gives us gifts. Paul writes regarding these spiritual gifts in 1 Corinthians 12. There are gifts of wisdom, knowledge, healing, miracles, prophecy, discerning of spirits, other tongues and the interpretation of tongues. The Holy Spirit also gives gifts of ministry: teaching, preaching, and organizing. He fills our lives with these gifts so that we may minister effectively for Him in this world, and enjoy His presence in sweet fellowship.

Early in my Christian life the Lord taught me to trust Him for wisdom and knowledge. While going to Bible college, I worked 10 hours each week for the school to help pay for my tuition. One day, Mrs. Barney, a school administrator, asked me, "Can you cook?" "I guess so," I answered. "Good," she said, "We need you to bake muffins for breakfast tomorrow."

Very early the next day, I awoke, got on my knees and prayed, "Lord, give me guidance." I had never made a muffin in my life. All the time I was mixing and baking, I was praying, "Lord, help me." The cook came to breakfast. To her surprise, we had the biggest and best muffins she had ever seen. This was an early lesson that has carried me through life. Look to the Holy Spirit for help and guidance.

Samson, by the power of the Holy Spirit, provided 30 changes of garments by killing 30 Philistines. When surrounded by the Philistine army in a town, he awoke in the middle of the night and walked off with the gates of the town. He slew 1000 Philistines with the jawbone of a donkey.

Delilah asked Samson, "Please tell me where your great strength lies…" (Judges 16:6). After much persuasion, Samson told her, "If I am shaven, then my strength will leave me, and I shall become weak, and be like any other man." While Samson slept on Delilah's lap, men came and cut his hair.

Was Samson's strength in his hair or in the abstinence of wine? Most assuredly not. Samson's power came by the Holy Spirit upon his life. However, the Holy Spirit only enabled him so long as he kept his Nazarite vow. Christians are committed to a life of separation to God. To be used of God, we must be kept by the Holy Spirit. This happens when we submit to God and look to Him for strength.

Samson had his eyes plucked out, and was fettered to a grinding stone. But the Bible says, "the hair of his head began to grow again" (Judges 16:22). Samson renewed his vows to God. The end came when the Philistines had a feast and brought Samson to make mockery of him and to show off their captive. Thousands of Philistines were on the roof of the building making merry. Samson placed his hands on the two main pillars of the building and prayed, "Lord, do it again." The pillars fell, the building collapsed, and thousands of Philistines were killed. Samson also died, but he died triumphantly.

Do not quench the Spirit (1 Thessalonians 5:19).

The Promises of God

Will you give me a teaching job next school year?" one of our graduates asked. "If I can, I will," I replied. "No, I want you to promise me," he said. The student looked bewildered. He didn't understand. I tried to explain that I do not know the circumstances of tomorrow and therefore cannot make a promise.

How different with God! His promises are "yea and amen." He knows the future and He speaks with certainty.

God made promises to Abraham in Genesis 12: The promise that His children would become a great nation, and that He would bless them.

God knows the future and
speaks with certainty.

Years went by and Abraham saw no children. Finally, when he was 99 years old, three angels visited him and told him he would have a son. His wife, listening inside the tent, laughed. "Ha, now that we are old and I'm beyond child-bearing age, shall we have pleasure?" God waited until it was seemingly impossible for Abraham and Sarah to have children. God wanted to show them that nothing is too hard for the Lord (Genesis 18:14).

God's promises to us are many. Here are a few of the most important, in my opinion. *He promises eternal life.* The Scriptures tell us that whosoever will call upon the name of the Lord will be saved. This is speaking of eternal life, a life that we will have with God forever. Death is not the end. It is only the end of this body as we know it. There is a new, richer, higher life waiting for those who have put their trust in Jesus. The gift of God is eternal life through Jesus Christ.

Another precious promise is *His presence.* At the end of Matthew's Gospel, Jesus gave the commission to go to the ends of the earth with the Good News. He said, "I will be with you till the end of the age."

God's presence makes us feel good. He comforts us. He gives us joy, love and peace. However, He is with us to help us in this present life. He keeps us from sinning. The Holy Spirit is our strength, our guide, our wisdom. He gives us courage. He leads us into Christian service. The Holy Spirit is our constant companion through life.

As God blessed Abraham, *He has promised to bless us.* Third John, verse 2, says that He wants us to prosper and be in health even as our souls prosper.

My attitude has always been, "Lord, bless my brother, but don't forget me." I rejoice whenever I see someone else getting blessed. It does my heart good. But I too want to know God's blessing. God told Abraham that He would be blessed and would be a blessing. That is my desire for Haiti.

Some people have taken this verse and pushed it to the extreme. Not every Christian will become rich, and as it were, drive a Cadillac. God's blessings encompass many things. It is good health, a good marriage and family life. It is to have enough to meet your needs and some left over to bless others.

When I see the poor of Haiti, my heart breaks. Poverty is not of God. It is a curse of the enemy. When I see strong young men sitting by the side of the road unable to find employment, my spirit grieves. Every person should have the dignity of employment, the ability to earn a living and have self-respect. Hunger, disease, poverty, ignorance and spiritual impoverishment comes from the devil. We need to do spiritual warfare, defeat the enemy, and bring liberty to the captives.

One of the great promises of God is that *He will return in bodily form* to this earth. He is coming, although we do not know when. Every day I pray, "Come quickly, Lord Jesus."

For all the promises of God in Him are Yes, and in Him Amen, to the glory of God through us (2 Corinthians 1:20).

God Works in Us and through Us

God gives men work to do. Since the very beginning when God placed Adam and Eve in the garden and told them to take care of it, men have enjoyed working. Inexplicably, man finds satisfaction and fulfillment in work.

It is hard, almost impossible, to separate the sacred from the secular. One does not have to be a preacher, a pastor, or evangelist to be doing God's work. All good work is God's work. In whatever way we earn an honest living, that is honorable work. The older trades, such as carpentry, animal herding, fishing, even motherhood, were considered sacred work.

God gives gifts to every person to fulfill his life's work. Intelligence, creativity, imagination, and perception are all gifts from God. The salesman, the engineer, and the artist are all gifted by God. The preacher has special gifts of communication; he is anointed so that his words take on special force. The presence of God is communicated by his every word.

It is a great joy to be used by God in this world.
It is a greater joy to feel Him at work in you,
making you into the person He wants you to be.

Each of us needs to come to know God's will for our lives and the good work that He has for us. "Now may the God of peace... make you complete in every good work to do His will, working in you what is well pleasing in His sight..." (Hebrews 13:20, 21). God is not only working through us, He is working in us. He is working in us what is pleasing in His sight.

The first work the Holy Spirit does in our lives is to regenerate us. When He comes into our lives we are "born again." The second work of the Spirit is to change us. We all have a human nature that has inclinations for the things of this world. From our spiritual inception the Holy Spirit begins to control our lives, making us into people who are pleasing in His sight. This is a supernatural work. The Holy Spirit lives within us, and He controls our actions and thereby changes us into the image of God's Son.

The work that Jesus did was vital. He preached, taught, healed the sick and did miracles. Finally, His greatest work was on the cross where He died for us, making the way for all men to be saved. But, the person of Jesus was just as important. He was tempted in all points, yet He was without sin. His sinless life was essential for our salvation. He is Jesus the man, but He is also the Christ, the eternal Son of God. The importance of His person cannot be separated from His work.

I give the leaders of the United States great credit in the way they have led our economy. Our economy is strong—a great work. For me, it is also important that a leader's life match the good work he or she may have done. We need leaders who are capable as executives. We also need leaders who are models to the nation. When our leaders fall morally, the nation hurts.

I have a dear friend who hitchhiked around the country after college, not knowing what to do in life. While picking pears in Oregon, a man gave him a book to read: *The Late Great Planet Earth*. In privacy he read the book and gave his life to Jesus. His life was changed. He is Ernie White, a great evangelist and pastor in Massachusetts.

It is a great joy to be used by God in this world. It is a greater joy to feel Him at work in you, making you into the person He wants you to be.

"Let your light so shine before men, that they may see your good works and glorify your Father in heaven" (Matthew 5:16).

Victory in Spiritual Warfare

Storms often come suddenly and unexpectedly: tornadoes, earth-quakes, hurricanes or even eruptions. Two calamities struck our mission in the fall of 1998. Hurricane Georges flooded our mission, leaving mounds of mud everywhere. Then in November, one of our school children drowned at the shore of our mission. Jesus told us that the Father "makes His sun rise on the evil and on the good and sends rain on the just and on the unjust" (Matthew 5:45). Here, sunshine speaks of good things that come. They come to everyone. The rain is paralleled to evil that likewise afflicts us all. Being in Christ does not isolate us from the evil that is in the world—nor does being outside of Christ exempt people from experiencing good things.

We need to be wise to the working of the devil,
and we must put on our spiritual armor.

Evil can show itself in many forms—war, famine, disease, drugs, strife, murder, theft. The list goes on, and it is long.

Personally, I am an idealist and a perpetual optimist. I believe that God is at work in the world, and that we are His instruments to bring salvation and change to the world. Along with my optimism, though, there is a good dose of realism. I know that we live in a fallen world and that evil will persist until Jesus returns. All previous attempts to build a utopia in this world have failed.

In the New Testament, evil is personified in the person of the devil. Jesus was tempted by the devil for forty days in the wilderness. As believers, we must realize that we are in a spiritual battle. Personally, I encounter spiritual warfare every day. The fiery darts of the enemy come. We need to be wise to the working of the devil, and we must put on our spiritual armor. I've often said, "I've not come to Haiti carrying a gun. Our weapons are not carnal; they are spiritual and mighty, through God defeating the enemy. Our weapons are truth, righteousness, faith, the Holy Spirit and the Word of God."

The danger is not the evil that is without that attacks us. The danger is the evil lurking in our hearts. Even as Job, believers today also have a hedge of protection around us. Satan cannot touch us. No harm can come to the believer from the enemy. Satan required special permission to touch Job. God granted it—because Job was to be a world example, for all time, of God's protection and goodness. That took place only once in history. God, my Father, is not about to give Satan liberty to touch me or any other believer. "The angel of the Lord encamps all around those who fear Him, and delivers them" (Psalm 34:7).

The danger is when the believer lets down his guard and enters into unrepented, willful sin. Then there is a breach in the hedge for the enemy to come in. Willful sin is like grabbing hold of the tail of a scorpion.

The believer grieves over both general and personal evil. We long to be free. We want God's Kingdom to come. But victory has already been won at the cross. The devil is defeated and salvation has come. Still, patience is needed. God is working out His will. Opportunity is still available for others to be saved. When that number is complete, He will return and all evil will be removed.

Therefore take up the whole armor of God, that you may be able to withstand in the evil day, and having done all, to stand (Ephesians 6:13).

The Wind of the Spirit

Which way is the wind blowing? Wind from the south often speaks of fair weather, and wind from the north, harsh weather. Spiritually speaking, we Christians do not regulate our lives by the weather. The circumstances of life are often contrary and would discourage us. "He who observes the wind will not sow..." (Ecclesiastes 11:4).

"I would go to the mission field, but I don't have the finances," is a common response. I have counseled many people to trust God. If God has called you to do a work for Him, then rest assured He will provide.

---

*God will work on your sanctification
wherever you are.*

"I don't have the proper training to serve God." We should prepare ourselves for a life of service but formal training isn't everything. I remember one seminary professor saying to me, "Peter didn't have much education, but I'd sure love to have him as my pastor."

"I'm too old to be of used to God." Age should never hinder us in the work of God. We have had a good number of older people, well into their 70's, come to Haiti. They worked hard, kept up with the young, and provided a great service for the Lord.

Some say, "Before we go to another country we should finish preaching the Gospel to everyone where we are." If we wait for everyone in our home country to hear the Gospel before we go, it will never happen. I believe we need to go to our Jerusalem, Judah, Samaria and the ends of the earth all at the same time.

If we wait until all our problems are solved or we're fully sanctified, we'll never go. Don't worry. God will work on your sanctification wherever you are.

Difficulties will always be with us. There are always contrary winds. We are always fighting the good fight of faith. These are opportunities to prove God. People who look to the wind are never prepared to sow. Those who let the wind of the Spirit blow on their lives are always busy planting and rejoicing in the good harvest the Lord gives.

―――――∞∞∞―――――

Those who let the wind of the Spirit blow on their lives are always busy planting and rejoicing in the good harvest the Lord gives.

―――――∞∞∞―――――

The wind blows where it wishes, and you hear the sound of it, but cannot tell where it comes from and where it goes. So is everyone who is born of the Spirit (John 3:8).

Our Purpose for Living

*T*he world is fraught with tensions. The Middle East remains volatile. Iraq resists U.N. inspections. The United States is caught up in one of the greatest moral crises in the history of the Union. The twenty-first century is already here. Some are predicting world calamity. The potential for economic problems for America looms great. A slowing economy, rising inflation and unemployment could bring demise to the present boom in America.

For me, problems have always plagued the world. True, in times past, they were often local. Now they could quickly engulf the world. As Christians we are stalwart. The next decade will bring problems. It will also, I believe, bring the greatest opportunity to share Jesus. We are ready to serve. We have received the power of the Holy Spirit (Acts 1:8). Witnesses will go to the end of the earth to bring the message of saving grace through Jesus Christ. It is not time to retreat, but to sound the alarm, to press the battle for the Lord.

When we begin to fulfill our purpose,
our lives become full of passion.

Some people are content to simply exist: to punch the clock and make it through. They go through the routine of life and with that they are content. Others strive to succeed. The fulfillment of the American dream for them is everything. Promotions, bigger homes and better cars are the marks of progress. This world for them is a playground of opportunity. Others, I believe, are looking to fulfill their purpose for being here on earth.

As a boy, I grew up as a Roman Catholic and went to catechism classes. I appreciate those early formative, basic teachings that I received in the church. I was taught that the purpose of man was *to know God, serve Him, and enjoy Him forever.* That is a wonderful, overriding truth. But the purpose of man also becomes specific. I was born to do what I am doing. I enjoy God now and I will enjoy Him forever. I believe that I was born to serve God in Haiti and in the Dominican Republic. God has a specific purpose for every believer. When we are ready to receive it, God will reveal it.

When we begin to fulfill our purpose, our lives become full of passion. We are excited with the prospect of what each new day will bring. We are ever peering over the horizon to catch a glimpse of what new thing God will bring into our lives. His purpose becomes larger than who we are, and fills our lives with zest and meaning. This becomes contagious. Those around us sense the presence of God and draw close to enter in, be a part, and follow.

God is always disclosing Himself and His desires for our lives. Yet we are not passive. Our place is to say "Yes," and to enter into God's purpose for our lives.

...being confident of this very thing, that He who has begun a good work in you will complete it until the day of Jesus Christ (Philippians 1:6).

Beyond Significance

"What will you do next with your life?" I am often asked. "Will you always be in Haiti?" Jeanne and I have been in Haiti since January of 1983. And as far into the future as I can see, we will be giving leadership to the work in Haiti. However, I have learned that the path of life is winding. I can see ahead—but only so far as the next bend in the road. Also, the curvature of the earth is such that a person, unless elevated, can only see five miles before the earth's curvature obstructs his view. What is coming over the horizon? What is around the bend? Isn't it wonderful that, from above, God has a bird's eye view? He sees the end as well as the beginning. Ours is not always to know, but to trust.

Many people have sought the path of success for themselves. Success is a driving force. The good life is often equated with achievement—academic, athletic, financial, performance, status or attainment in one's field of involvement. Some of this is healthy, normal and good. The danger is when it is pursued to the exclusion or neglect of spiritual, family, or personal development. Most people who make success life's goal end up disappointed. How sad when at the latter part of life we realize that the energies we spent on self only robbed us of any worthy achievement. Success, of itself, in the end is disappointing. Jesus illustrated this with the man whose barn was full, and repeatedly built bigger barns to fill (Luke 12:18-21). The man said to himself, "'...take your ease; eat, drink, and be merry.' But God said to him, 'You fool! This night your soul will be required of you.' So he is who lays up treasures for himself and is not rich toward God."

---⬯⬯⬯---

Move beyond success to significance.

---⬯⬯⬯---

Some people come to the realization that life is short and they want to move on to do something significant while here on earth. New goals are set. Now the determination is to live for others rather than self. The new motto is, "The key to fulfillment is to do something that has significance." Now time, which is life, is used along with energies and money to work with children or youth-mentoring, the aged, the imprisoned, or the homeless. The list is endless. Former President Jimmy Carter is involved with Habitat for Humanity. Their slogan is "No more shacks." Enormous amounts of money has been given for schools, hospitals, and civic improvement. John D. Rockefeller, a man of strong Christian conviction, gave fortunes for medical research.

Jesus told a story in Matthew 25 of a man who had great possessions and went on a long journey. The man entrusted his goods to servants. His goods were likened to talents. At the time of Jesus, a talent was a measure of money, approximately $1,000. Clearly, the man who went on the journey represents Jesus, and we are His servants to whom He has entrusted His goods. Some servants were given five talents, some two, but all were given at least one. The people with the five and two talents doubled theirs. The person with one talent hid his in the ground. Those who invested their talents and doubled them were rewarded: "Well done, good and faithful servant...Enter into the joy of your lord." The one who hid his talent was reprimanded, "You wicked and lazy servant," and was cast out. Some people waste their lives living only to succeed; others want to invest their lives in something significant.

All of us have a responsibility to use the gifts with which God has endowed us for the benefit of others and the extension of His kingdom. Invest for the Master—move on beyond success to significance—what is beyond significance?

Some people live to exist, others live to succeed and still others want to do something significant with their lives, but what is beyond significance?

Life is short at best. Some people realize that and begin to ask, "Why am I here?" Is it only to accumulate and consume? Or is there more? Some people begin to look for something significant to do. This is done in hopes of finding fulfillment, a purpose, a reason for living. Some people begin to use their abilities, time and resources to help others. It may be in the form of working with the elderly, giving money to a worthy cause, feeding the hungry or building homes for the homeless.

Let me say that in and of itself success is not an evil. We all want to do well in our area of endeavor. We wish our children well. Hard work and the desire for success has brought development to the world. We are not as the Buddhists striving to rid ourselves of all desire.

The thing that can go awry with success is when that is what we live for. If all we want out of life is to accumulate all we can and enjoy all we have, then we have hit a brick wall. The same is true with doing something significant. Yes, there are virtues in helping those who are less fortunate than us. But we are not humanitarians. Significance should not be the driving, compelling force of our lives. And we do not live this life looking for fulfillment. That is a vain attempt.

What then do we live for?

Beyond significance there is submission.

Beyond significance there is submission. I have not gone to Haiti and spent the last 17 years of my life there preaching, building and educating to find fulfillment. I went to Haiti because God sent me there. From the day I came to faith in Jesus Christ I knew that I was going to the mission field. However, God never asked me where I wanted to go. If He did, I probably would have chosen the town in Italy where my parents came from. Surely, the good food of Italy would have allured me. Rather, God did not ask me. He sent me. From the day I came to know God, He told me who I was to be, where I was to go, and what I was to do. God invaded my life and took over.

There are many examples of this in Scripture. I think it is humorous when people today want to be an apostle. Do you know what they do with apostles? They beat them, lock them in jail, cut off their heads, boil them in oil and crucify them upside down. God chooses His apostles. Paul was one of them. He was apprehended on the Damascus road. He was a chosen vessel. At the end of his life he said he was "obedient to the heavenly vision" (Acts 26:19).

Abraham was told to leave home and country. When he was 99 years of age, finally, a message was given to him that "Sarah shall have a son..." (Genesis 18:10). What a blessing Issac was—the child of promise. Then, when the child had grown, God tested Abraham and told him to "take your son Issac whom you love and offer him as a burnt offering" (Genesis 22:2). Abraham went with the wood and fire to the appointed mountain, built an altar, bound his son, drew the knife, and when he was about to cut the throat of his son, an angel said, "Stay your hand, now I know you fear me" (Genesis 22:12). Was Abraham looking for success or to do something significant? No! He was in submission to God.

The greatest example is Jesus. "Lo, in the volume of the book I have come to do your will, O God" (Hebrews 10:7). In the garden of Gethsemane, He cried, "If it be possible, let this cup pass from me, nevertheless not my will but yours be done." Paul wrote of Jesus, "He was obedient, unto death, even the death of the cross."

The writer of Ecclesiastes said it all: "The whole duty of man is to fear God and keep His commandments" (12:7). Beyond significance there is submission.

> "Do not lay up for yourselves treasures on earth, where moth and rust destroy and where thieves breaks in and steal; but lay up for yourselves treasures in heaven, where neither moth nor rust destroys and where thieves do not break in and steal. For where treasure is, there your heart will be also" (Matthew 6:19-21).

The Essence of Christianity

A young man in the prime of his life died at approximately 30 years of age. He died a cruel death.

It was at the time of the Roman Empire. Rome would not tolerate rebellion on the part of the cities and the nations it conquered. Those who opposed were nailed naked to a tree and left exposed to the elements. It was a message to every one—don't mess with Rome.

A young man named Jesus was tried by a Roman governor and His accusers asked for Him to be hung on a tree—crucified. The young man said that His life was not being taken from Him, but rather He was giving it—as the means of salvation for the whole world. His life was being offered as a sacrifice for sin.

The natural man would recoil, "What a waste," they would say. At the prime of life He was crucified. For the natural man the cross was an enigma—a contradiction—a foolish thing. The Bible clearly says "The preaching of the cross to them who perish is foolishness, but to us who are saved it is the power of God. 1 Corinthians 1:18"

The cross is the very heart of Christianity. Without the cross and the resurrection Christianity would be reduced to every other religion in the world. The essence of Christianity is sacrifice.

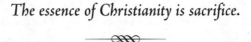

The essence of Christianity is sacrifice.

Jesus gave His life and we are called to give ours.

America has always been able to call upon its young people to defend the nation and be willing to die for the principles we stand for— life, liberty, and the pursuit of happiness. If America ever gets so caught up in the pursuit of self and pleasure; forgets the principles upon which our nation has been built and becomes unwilling to fight and die for them, then we will begin to decline as a nation.

The Roman Empire declined because the people lost faith in Greek and Roman mythology. When their faith was gone they began to live for self. The empire had become wealthy. They hired other nations to fight their battles. The rest is history.

Christianity calls for its disciples to give their lives for the cause of spreading the news of Jesus Christ. One of the threats to the church is the prosperity of America. Secularism is a creeping force, invading every home. Pleasure-seeking numbs the spirit and dilutes the soul. Success in and of itself is not an evil. God wants us to succeed—but when it becomes the all-inclusive reason for living it brings dry rot to spiritual bones. "If you saw my beautiful home, you'd know why I can't become a missionary," one woman said to me. Elisha killed the oxen and burned his plow when the prophetic mantle fell on him.

The secret to the abundant life is death to self. Jesus said, "Unless a grain of wheat falls into the ground and dies it remains alone; but if it dies it produces much grain. He who loves his life will lose it and he who hates his life in this world will keep it for eternal life" (John 1: 24, 25).

Sacrifice is the key for vitality in the church. Believers in Jesus must be willing to give their all to follow Him. The youth of America need to hear again the words of Jesus, "Come. Follow Me." And then go to the poor, the oppressed of the world and bring Jesus. Service to God always entailed sacrifice. You may be sent somewhere and be out of touch with the rest of the world because of the lack of communication. The living conditions may be primitive and facilities poor or almost non-existent. But go you must.

Free—Set Free

Greatness ultimately is shown by how we treat other people. We consider love to be the greatest virtue. Yet, love is not an abstraction. It is always demonstrated in the context of another person. Nehemiah was a truly great man. We know him for rebuilding the Temple and the walls around Jerusalem.

Now I want you to see another aspect of his character. In the fifth chapter of Nehemiah, he dealt with the oppression of Jews by their fellow brethren. In Israel it was a time of economic difficulty and many Jews could not meet their financial obligations. They were forced to mortgage their homes and sell their lands. When this action did not suffice, they began selling their children into slavery to other Jews.

Today, in America, I'm afraid that many people are being lulled into a false sense of security and are selling themselves into financial bondage. Times are good, most people are working and many families have two or three incomes. The message of the new economics is being preached. The message says: Because of the expanding global markets and the ability of the Federal Reserve to control the economy, we are no longer subject to boom-bust business cycles. The good times will only get better continually.

Personally, I have no problem believing that God has blessed us with good times. What troubles me is when all restraint is thrown out the window. Many people are hocked to the hilt. When one credit cards gets filled up, they get another. Many people have re-mortgaged their homes and have been enticed to take a cruise, buy a new sports car. One television advertisement encouraged, "re-mortgage your home and buy a hot stock." The Scriptures, it seems to me, teach that during good times we should store up for bad times. "Be a debtor to no man" would help all of us.

As believers, God, through Christ, has set us free from every spiritual ensnarement. In the Old Testament freedom was also liberty from financial problems. The man who is over extended financially is not a free man and is prone to destruction at any moment. The people providing easy money may appear friendly, but if you are unable to make your payments on time, these same people can become your oppressor. I write to encourage you to be debt-free.

The people who were financially oppressed came to Nehemiah and cried, "Let us get grain that we may eat and live (verse 2)." Nehemiah called an assembly. He rebuked the nobles and rulers, "each of you is extracting usury from his brother…what you are doing is not good. Restore to them this day their lands, vineyards, houses, children and money." A great day occurred. The rulers answered, "We will restore it and require nothing from them (verse 12). Spiritual revival broke out, "All the congregation said, 'Amen' and praised the Lord (verse 13).

It is important how we treat other people. We should never oppress. Our ministry is to set people free.

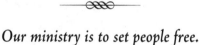

Our ministry is to set people free.

We have young men and women at our mission who at one time had nothing. Today, they know Jesus, are well educated and enjoy good employment. I urge you to be as Nehemiah and set the oppressed free.

Finish the Race

*I*t is easy to run up a flag. It is more difficult to keep it flying. This is applicable to everything. It is especially true for the believer in the race of life.

Many young people come to spend a week at our mission. When they're about to leave, I often wonder where they will be 10, 20 or 30 years from now. Many, I know, will go on to live a full life of service to Jesus Christ. My heartfelt desire is for them to run well the race and finish the course. Paul said, "I have finished the race" (2 Timothy 4:7). For me, I've been running for 46 years, but I've not yet finished. I've a way to go, and perhaps more hurdles to jump.

Hebrews 12:1 and I Corinthians 9:24 tell us how to run the race.

1. *Lay aside every weight.* A runner in a race goes as light as possible. Light shorts and a tank top are all he wants, and shorts without pockets are best.

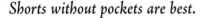

Shorts without pockets are best.

No runner wants to carry an unnecessary load. Even the lightest load carried over a great distance becomes heavy. Paul no doubt saw the Grecian athletes in contest and used what he saw to illustrate the Christian life. How best to run? No extra weights! It is easy to encumber our lives with things that distract and hinder us from being our best for the Lord. We are all different and what may hinder one person may not bother another. A weight is not necessarily something wrong. It may simply distract, and, as it were, slow us down.

By way of illustration, golf for one person may be a great diversion and form of exercise and help the believer in his life. To another person, it could become an obsession, a distraction and a great weight. Every known negative is to be put out of our lives. A clean mind will lead to a clean heart. Paul is simply saying "run light" so that we may run well.

Obligations, duties and responsibilities are natural in life. We never want to shirk from them. But we all know that too much responsibility can turn into a weight that hinders us in the race of life. Many of us are too busy. Family life can be hurt by too many activities. This tends to be one of my problems—too much good to do, often to the neglect of the truly more important. I preach, "Take time to smell the roses," but fail to practice what I preach. Anything that hinders us in our Christian walk has to go.

2. *Next, the writer of Hebrews mentions sin that ensnares us.* Some things are a definite No! No! Willful sin, the violation of God's Word, will bring guilt. Not only will sin hinder you from running, you may find yourself flat on your face. The desire of the enemy is to make us ineffectual. Sin will do it every time. Christianity is not adherence to a creed or a set of teachings. Ultimately, it is a life lived. The only remedy for sin is repentance and to allow God, by His Spirit, to reign over our lives. His presence brings health, peace, joy; these give us strength to run well.

3. *Run with endurance.* We are not sprint runners. We are running a marathon. We need to pace ourselves to go the distance. Personally, I'm a builder. And some days I only lay one brick. But I plod on, and in time, amazing things take place. For most of us, the race is not over in a day. It takes a lifetime.

4. *Looking unto Jesus.* He is our strength, our motivator and sustainer. We look to Him. He is the author and the finisher of our

faith. Jesus placed us in this race. This is of His doing and He will not allow us to fail. He is also the finisher. He is now working in us—and will complete the work.

"He who has begun a good work in you will complete it" (Philippians 1:6).

And Yet There Is More

*H*ave you ever received a trophy or an award recognizing your achievements? Oscars are given yearly in the film industry for best films, acting, music, writers and producers. Athletes are awarded gold, silver and bronze medals, trophies and awards. Businessmen are often recognized with plaques.

What about the believer? Is the faithful Christian ever recognized? The reward of the servant of God is the fruits of his labor. Here in Haiti the thing that gives me my greatest joy is when someone comes to faith in Christ and then goes on to grow in the Lord. These are all the trophies I need in this world.

And yet there is more. When General Dwight D. Eisenhower returned to the United States after destroying the German army in Europe, he was given a hero's welcome. When his plane arrived, signs saying "Welcome Home Ike" greeted him. A ticker tape parade in New York City gave him a grand reception. At the same time that General Eisenhower came home, a missionary returned from Africa. He had spent many years there. His wife died and was buried in Africa. Now, because of broken health, the missionary society would not send him back to Africa.

"Boy," he said to a friend, feeling a little sorry for himself, "when I came from Africa no one greeted me." Then his friend turned and said, "Yes, but you're not home yet!" The reward of God's servants in this world are the fruit of their labors. Yet, there is more.

To us will be given the crown of eternal life. Paul, thinking of the Grecian races said, "We do not labor for a crown that will perish— but for an incorruptible one" (1 Corinthians 9:25).

To us will be given the crown of eternal life.

Jesus, in the parable of the talents (Matthew 25) spoke of those who labored: "Well done, good and faithful servant. You have been faithful in a little, I will make you ruler over much, enter into the joy of your Lord."

Paul, saying farewell to Timothy, said, "I have fought the good fight. I have finished the race. I have kept the faith. There is laid up for me the crown of righteousness" (2 Timothy 4:7, 8).

The pure pleasure of seeing God's face will be beyond description.

For me there is nothing more meaningful than the assurance that I have eternal life. It is hard to imagine that we will be with God forever. In this world we are richly rewarded, and yet there is more.

Is Globalization a Sign of the Time?

Globalization is a fact of life. It involves world trade, the availability of information and the electronic transfer of funds. Trade has become vital to all the nations of the world. Information on almost everything is available on the Worldwide Web, and many people are experiencing the transfer of funds electronically. Social security does not send checks to private homes, so if you collect social security, you must have a bank account where they send your funds.

Part of the process of globalization is the consolidation of monies. An amazing thing has taken place in Europe. Eleven countries have come together to form one currency—the Euro dollar. Not too far in the past, nationalism would have prevented such a move. This union will soon continue beyond the finances and will reach into the politics. Some people dream of a United Europe.

Now in America, talk is strong about having one currency that would include all the countries from Canada in the north to Argentina at the southern end of South America. Impossible, some would say. That was said of Europe. Strong forces are now at work to bring it about.

At the same time, there is talk of the need for one currency in Asia, which would include countries such as Japan, Korea, Malaysia, Singapore, Taiwan, Thailand, Vietnam and the Philippines.

Economic ties through world trade agreements and financial loans are taking place everywhere. Even so, just as there are mergers of companies taking place in Europe on a regular basis, everyday we hear of another merger. Through satellites, global communication has become instantaneous. The world is changing and it will never be the same again.

I am reminded of the teaching I received back in Bible school. We were taught that financial transactions would one day require a mark of identity on either the hand or forehead. I was taught that Europe would come together again as a revival of the Roman Empire. Is what is happening today a sign that the coming of the Lord is soon?

Many scholars have said that the world was prepared for the first coming of Jesus. Without the Roman Empire in place, the Scriptures would not have been fulfilled. The means of controlling the masses of people that Rome conquered was by nailing dissidents to a cross. The cross was Rome's means of capital punishment. Therefore, when Jesus was arrested and tried by the Roman governor, He was sentenced to crucifixion. Also, Rome brought peace to the earth. The power of the empire brought "Pax de Roman." This made travel safe and the spread of the Gospel possible.

What is our reaction to all of this? Do we run to the hills to hide? Do we live in fear? Never.

We are to be faithful, even until death.

We are to be faithful, even until death. Jesus said, "Labor, for the night will come when no one can work" (John 9:4). Is the world now quickly being prepared for the second coming of Jesus?

In the light of what is happening in the world, we Christians need to put aside our differences. Why do we let doctrines and denominations separate us? Let us come together. We are one in Christ. Let us become strong in the Spirit, quicken the pace of our labors, and bring the message of the saving grace of our Lord Jesus to the whole world in our generation.

Just Stand Still

Over the years I have not said much about spiritual warfare, nor have I written about it. But, I have been engaged in spiritual warfare. Heavy. I have fought and won.

After Moses died, Joshua was chosen to lead the nation of Israel. His task was to lead the Israelites into the promise land. Joshua was a warrior. Many battles lay before him. The greatest was his first. The city of Jericho lay directly in his path. It had to be taken to begin to secure the land.

God had given clear instruction on how to take the city. March about it in silence once a day for six days. Then on the seventh with the priests leading carrying the ark of the covenant, they were to march around Jericho seven times, face the walls, blow the trumpets and shout. Hebrews 11:30 says "By faith the walls fell down."

At Ai, the next town to be taken, the Israelites suffered defeat. "Why, Lord?" Joshua asked. There had been disobedience. Gold, silver, precious items were stolen at Jericho. One man's sin caused defeat in battle.

Our task is not to beat the devil. Our task is to obey God. The Lord fights our battles. In fact, the battle was won at the cross, where Jesus died for us. He arose from the dead, victor over sin, death and the devil. His victory is our victory. We simply appropriate the finished work of the cross.

When Moses fled Egypt, the Egyptian army was in hot pursuit of him and the nation of run-away slaves. The situation appeared perilous. The Red Sea was before them and a furious Pharoah behind. The people of God began to languish, "It would have been better for us to remain in Egypt. Moses…let us alone," they said. "Do not be afraid, stand still and see the salvation of the Lord. God will fight for you," Moses replied (Exodus 14:12-14). With His mighty hand God opened the Red Sea and brought the people to the other side. There they stood and watched the Egyptian army perish as the sea crashed down upon them.

Some people think that spiritual warfare is done by shouting at the devil, or by speaking loudly to God. All our denouncing or invoking will accomplish nothing if we are not living in obedience to God.

The secret to victory, which may include longevity, good health, prosperity and success in life or in ministry, is doing what God expects and asks of us.

The secret to victory, which may include longevity, good health, prosperity and success in life or in ministry, is doing what God expects and asks of us.

"If you dance, you have to pay." This is a saying that I heard many years ago. It is the image of a fiddler playing a tune. If a person dances to the fiddler's music, naturally, the dancer should reward the musician. The devil, too, fiddles and wants people to dance to his music. The problem is, if you dance to his music, he will demand payment. And pay you will. The devil does not ask for payment—he extracts payment. I don't dance nor do I flirt with the devil.

Rather, we are to dance to the music of the Lord. He is the Lord of the dance. His music brings wholeness and strength to our lives. It is refreshing and sweet. By the presence of the Holy Spirit we are able to submit to God and live in victory.

One in Christ

A favorite theme of mine is our oneness in Jesus Christ. In capsule form I share it with visiting groups that come to Haiti. One of my motives is to bring unity to the diverse groups that come to our mission. New Missions has taken a non-denominational stance. Therefore, people from many church backgrounds come to work at our mission. Often in any one group people from several church backgrounds are represented.

My position is, if you confess Christ as your Savior, then you are my brother or sister.

If you confess Christ as your Savior,
then you are my brother or sister.

You are not a half-brother—but a full brother! What I mean by that is my fellowship with you is not based on theology. We agree on the essential teachings of Scripture. But, your theology does not have to line up perfectly with mine for us to have fellowship.

I do not look for a political union of the different church groups. Rather, I consider that we are already one in Christ. According to 1 Corinthians 12 we are different members but all parts of the one body of which Christ is the head. I tease and say—you may have your pet doctrine and enjoy patting your pet. But when you come to New Missions we lay aside our differences, recognize our oneness in

Christ and come together to worship, preach the gospel and work together.

The New Testament believers never called themselves by denominational names. No, they were called "Christians" (Acts 11:26). I would prefer that people say I am a Christian who is serving the Lord in a particular denomination. This shows their confession of faith.

Denominationalism has served the Lord well. However, when it separates Christians, when it hinders us from coming together to worship, when it keeps us from doing evangelism and bringing the truth of Jesus to the world, then it is wrong.

At New Missions we did not want to export the denominationalism of America to Haiti. If you enter any of our 10 churches and ask any believer what they are, they'll respond, "I'm a Christian."

All believers have received the Holy Spirit when they were regenerated. I also recognize that we are all in different places in life in the Spirit. And only God knows the heart and the true spiritual place of the believer. I would encourage you to be convinced from the scriptures of your biblical position. Then I would encourage you to respect and appreciate the position of every other brother and sister in Christ. Then come together as one to worship and do the work of our Lord. Listen to what Paul said: "The body is one and has many members, but all the members of that body, being many are one body, so also is Christ" (2 Corinthians 12:12).

There Is Healing

*T*he present state of man is both glorious and ignominious. We enjoy the good life—God, family, friends, success, good food, and the conveniences that modern life brings, and yet it will all be taken away—all, except God. We live in a body that is both wonderful and yet destined for old age. It will wear out like a garment. Sickness comes, whether it is a headache, the flu or something as serious as cancer. The latest statistic on cancer is that one out of every three Americans will come down with cancer and one in six will die from it.

Thank God that we are promised—one day, a new body. That will be glorious. But, what do we do until then?

We are one person, a composite of body, soul and spirit, and what affects one part of us affects the others. A healthy mind helps to bring about a healthy body. And of course if we are healthy spiritually, it affects the whole man. This is why right conduct is necessary for good health. We cannot violate our sense of what is right and wrong without affecting the entire person. For me, good health begins with a good relation with God and then allowing that relationship to guide our conduct. Peace and happiness is connected to our physical well-being, which is affected by our thoughts and deeds. The different parts of man are inter-related. Any one affects the others. God's desire for us is clearly stated in John's prayer for us in his third letter, verse two, "Beloved, I pray that you may prosper in all things and be in health, just as your soul prospers."

We never want to hold on to this world too long. The believer in Jesus has no fear of death. For death is only a passage from this world into another world. Paul the Apostle said, "to be absent from the body is to be present with the Lord" (2 Corinthians 5:8).

Sickness can work to remind us of our mortality and to help place things in their proper perspective. Sickness can be a glorious opportunity to know our Lord in a greater depth. His grace is exceeding, it far outweighs any suffering, pain or problem. Sickness also opens the door for us to see God work a miraculous healing in our bodies. Healing can come instantly and completely.

Faith says, "If I can but touch the hem of His garment, I will be whole." Faith is born in our hearts. It is the ability to look beyond what is in this realm and look into the realm of God and see His love, compassion and power and say, "Yes—Jesus can heal me."

The woman with the ulcerated body, Matthew 9:20, felt unworthy to call attention to herself. In her heart she said, "I'll touch, be healed and no one will know." She planned to leave silently. In the midst of a crowd she stooped, reached and touched—only the hem of Jesus' garment. Immediately He felt virtue go out of Him and asked, "Who touched me?" No doubt, she was a simple woman, uneducated, of little or no stature in life. She had no wealth, no position, no power and yet she was a woman of faith. And that day she stole a blessing.

Most of the people that Jesus healed had a pathetic illness. What I mean by pathetic is that their condition was extreme and humanly impossible. For example, blind Bartimaeus. He was pathetic. The lepers, they were pathetic. The woman with the oozing ulcer. She was pathetic. They were pathetic, but not beyond the reach of God. No one, no sickness, no circumstances, no problem is beyond the healing touch of our Lord.

At thirteen I began stuttering and this continued into college. I had a problem diagnosed as stop plosive. I could not say five words together in a sentence without binding up and becoming unable to speak. For this affliction I cried to the Lord. I knew that He had called me to preach. The entire Christian community that I was related to united and prayed for me and God set me free. I've enjoyed more than 40 years of preaching and teaching with great liberty.

I know firsthand—God is my healer. My God is able for anything. Healing is for you. If God is alive and He is the creator of all there is, then there is nothing beyond what He can do. Jesus said, "Ask and it will be given to you" (Matthew 7:7).

Some Truths About God

God is there. For me the Lord is at the very core of my being. Some people want proof that God exists before they will commit their life to Him. Like a scientist looking into a microscope they want to gather data to prove God. Others go on a philosophical binge and think that by reasoning they will discover God. Clearly, by searching, man cannot find God. God rather has come to us. He has made Himself known. Jesus has come and He has shown us the Father.

God has never set out to prove His existence. The scripture says, "In the beginning God created the heavens and the earth." Ours is simply to believe. True, this life is precious. Never deny it, but it is fleeting. One day it will be over—what then? For me, I feel the Spirit of God within me. His presence gives me assurance that there is life beyond this life of greater dimensions, proportions and opportunities. The great gift of God is eternal life. He is my God here, and one day, I will go to be with Him there.

Some people struggle to enter into God's presence. They talk about going beyond the veil into the holy of holies. Well, I have good news—the veil in the temple was rent in two. Now we are in His full presence.

The Old Testament tabernacle is a picturesque example of how God dwelt in the midst of the Israelite people. Today we have a "better" relationship with God. He no longer dwells in structures built by man. When we receive Jesus as our Lord and Savior He comes and dwells in us. Paul said, "You are the dwelling place of God" (2 Corinthians 6:16). There is nothing that separates us from the full presence of God—no building, no veil, no priesthood, no ritual. I'll use a double negative for emphasis. No—Nothing!

God cares. I love the good times when everything is going well. The holidays, birthdays and anniversaries are special. But what do we do when our boat begins to rock? Perhaps some part of our body begins to wear out or breakdown, what do we do then? What do we do when we lose a loved one, or our finances hit bottom and we don't have enough to pay our bills? Push the panic button? Question the existence of a caring God? Criticize and bemoan our lot in life? Or do we come closer to God, rely on His wisdom and draw on His strength?

Is it possible to turn Christianity into a religion? What was intended to be a life-giving relationship can become another set of rules, dogmas and obligations only to bind us into a form that we call Christianity. Have you ever opened a clam only to find that there was nothing inside the shell? Have you ever been served a bowl of soup— that had no stock, only water with bouillon-cube flavor? We can have all the right sayings, songs and settings and not have the real thing. Christianity is more than going to church. The Lord intended that we would have a relationship with Him that would bring about an abundant life.

As we serve God, we come to know Him better. He does befriend us. He is our life companion. He does help us. He is the One who comes alongside. He does answer prayer. He knows the desires of my heart and delights to answer when I call upon Him. God is not some abstract force who is disconnected, disassociated or disinterested in us. He is there—personal—and working on our behalf. It's great. I love Him.

Talents: From and For the Lord—Part 1

*E*ach of us have been given abilities—talents that enable us to function effectively. Everyone has at least one talent, some people are loaded with them. When we think of talents, what do we think of—often art, music, sports. True, Tiger Woods and Andre Boccelli have great talent, but so do the rest of us, often in many different areas.

Isn't it wonderful that we're all different. Foolishly, at some time, we've probably all thought, "If everyone were like me, what a wonderful world it would be." But God loves variety, and no two of anything are alike. There will never be another person just like you, not unless you are cloned before you die. Each of us were created to make a unique contribution and in a special way reflect God's love.

Talents cannot be produced. They do not come about by training, they are God-given. They are part of us, even as our DNA, they are in our genes. Our younger son Timothy at a very young age showed natural skills on the piano. I insisted that he take piano lessons. Today, he plays keyboard for a large singles' ministry and for worship on Sunday. When we attempt to get people to function outside of their talents we program them for failure. On the other hand, everyone will be a success when their talents are discovered and put to good use.

Talents enable people to become teachers, engineers, doctors, businessmen, mechanics—the list is endless. These abilities are used to earn a living, and support the work of God. "A man's gift makes room for him" (Proverbs 18:16). Many people go to a third world country, such as Haiti, pay their own way, and then use their gift to bless a people who have not had the same opportunities. There is something rewarding about doing something for someone who cannot give anything in return.

Service to God is one of the apexes of the Christian life. A mountain often has several peaks. Spiritually speaking, I'm not sure which one is the greatest, probably worship, but for sure Christian service is one of them. We are all called to serve the Lord. The example is Jesus—with basin and towel He washed the feet of the Apostles and left us an example, and in myriad ways we are to go into the world to share Jesus and wash feet.

In Matthew25 Jesus gave three parables concerning His coming. The first is the ten virgins, five with oil and five without. The lesson is—be prepared. The second parable is the talents given to the servants of a man who went on a long journey. Here the lesson is—we are all given responsibilities and we will be held accountable for them. Third, Jesus gave the parable of the separation of the sheep and goats. Here the lesson is—the basis of judgment is service to God. "I was hungry," Jesus said, "thirsty, naked, in prison, sick and you came and ministered to me." The disciples asked, "When did we do these things?" Jesus answered, "In that you did it to the least, you did it to me." Let us use our days to the full in service to God.

Talents: From and For the Lord—Part 2

The truth of our Lord's return is precious to every believer. We pray, "Come quickly, Lord" (Revelations 3:11). In response to the apostles' inquiry, Jesus gave the conditions (signs) that will proceed His return to this earth. "False Christs, wars, famines, earthquakes, and tribulation would come," Jesus said. "As it was in the days of Noah...so will it be when the Son of Man returns" (Matthew 24).

Most of us have received teaching regarding Christ's second coming and are thankful for it. Some people become quite concerned about the nature of His coming—the how or when. Because some have believed that His coming was imminent—at the door they have felt that there was no time for sharing the Gospel or working for the Kingdom. What time we have must be spent in sanctifying our hearts, that we may be pure at His coming, is often the attitude. This can be a great danger. Inactivity is not the nature of God nor His desire. Jesus taught, "Occupy until I come" (Luke 19:13).

Let us grasp well the teachings of the twenty-fourth chapter of Matthew and then move on into the twenty-fifth chapter. In this chapter there are three stories, which round out our Lord's teaching regarding His second coming.

The first is the story of ten virgins, five wise and five foolish. Attendants often accompanied the bridegroom into the place of festivities at a wedding. They did this with lighted lamps. When the cry came, "the bridegroom cometh," five virgins were prepared with lighted lamps. The other five ran to buy oil. They were too late—the door to the feast was locked. The message is clear—be ready. When we receive Jesus as our Saviour the Holy Spirit comes into our lives, our lamps are lit, and we are ready for the Lord's return.

The second story Jesus told is that of the talents. A man went on a long journey and left the responsibilities of his estate to his servants. The responsibilities were called talents. In Jesus' day, a talent was a measure of money. Our Lord has gone and He has given the responsibility of the Kingdom to us, His servants. Angels will not come to do the work of God. After the Master returned, the servants gave an account, those who were faithful had doubled the value of the master's household. They were bid well done, faithful servant. The person with one talent hid it and was sent out in disgrace. All of us are given areas of responsibility. To the measure that we are faithful in this world we will be given responsibilities in the world to come.

The last story that Jesus told was of the sheep and goats—one placed on the right, the other on the left. This was judgment and was based on the kindness shown to others by His servants. "I was hungry and you gave Me something to eat; I was thirsty, and you gave Me drink. I was a stranger, and you invited Me in, naked and you clothed Me, sick and you visited Me. I was in prison and you came to Me. When Lord did we do these things they asked. In that you did it to the least, you did it to Me" (verse 40). "Come, blessed of My Father, inherit the Kingdom" (verse 33).

Jesus our great example with basin and towel-washed feet. As His servants, we are to follow His example, and go into all the world and in a hundred different ways—wash feet.

Fuller Than Full

Christian service is where God wants to lead every believer. "I came not to be ministered unto but to minister," Jesus said. And Christ is the model for our lives. Jesus quoted Isaiah 61:1 and Luke 4:18 "I am anointed to…." Everything He said that followed was service. The anointing is for service. Acts 1:8 is a verse so loved and often quoted, "You shall receive power when the Holy Spirit has come upon you, and you shall be witnesses to Me…to the ends of the earth."

We find our fulfillment in God's presence. My life is full when I'm full of His presence. He is everything to us and spiritually speaking, all we'll ever need. With God's presence, I am fully complete—out fishing or on the golf course. I have often said, I don't have to do anything—except what He asks me to do. However, God doesn't lead us into indolence, selfish living or carelessness. God has a work for each of us.

Obedience in service makes us fuller than full. We are full in Christ, yet when we allow Him to use us we are full by His presence, and then full because we labor for Him. There is deep fulfillment in being used of God. What a difference. Huge.

There is more than enough ministry for every believer to be occupied. And the myriad of ministries provides opportunity for every gift to find expression. I know of one church that has over 150 ministries functioning that people can involve themselves in, such as prison, elderly, youth, children, unwed mothers, addictions, motorcycle clubs—even a ministry group for those investing in equities.

Danger. The danger of not being involved in Christian service is drying up spiritually. As we give we receive. When we do not give we are in danger of drying up—a plum can quickly become a prune. The healthy Christian is the one involved.

Some people never feel adequate for Christian service. We are all human—and prone to human weakness. Some want to sit and be ministered to, then someday when they are built up sufficiently, then they will do something for God. In fact, the day we come to faith in Jesus we should begin to be involved. Don't waste years feeling inadequate. God wants to use you now. And of course, we continue to grow and learn and commit; that is a life-long process. As God works through us, He works in us. I have found that the best place for personal growth is in the work of God. Satisfied are we when we are fuller than full.

A Golden Opportunity

A millennium is a thousand years. In the book of Revelation, chapter 20, the scriptures tell of a thousand years of peace that will come to earth. This is not a time that will come about by human planning or international development. It will come about by God. In verse four, it says that, "Christ shall reign for a thousand years." Much discussion has taken place as to when and how this will take place. There are several differing positions. What we all agree upon is— good times will come upon the earth.

As Christians we believe that the world and human nature has been affected by the fall—Adam and Eve. The ground and man were cursed. True, Jesus has come, He has died for our salvation. Yet redemption is not complete. It will be complete when Jesus returns to earth. Then there will be a new world and we shall be changed in a moment. A glorious day is coming and we live in anticipation of it.

What do we do now—in the interim, between Christ's first and second coming? Do we segregate ourselves, bemoan our lot in life, curse the darkness and live in fear of the future?

That is not the message of our Savior. Jesus taught that we are the light, salt and yeast of the world. We are to permeate every strata of our world with a message of change and hope. As yeast effects the whole loaf of bread, we are to effect our world for good. Christians are true idealists. We not only speak of what is in the world, we also speak of what the world can become by God's help. We work to bring about a better day.

The unknown, the uncertain and the uncontrollable can bring fear unless we have a prior greater certainty in our lives. Our faith in

God makes us unmovable. The winds may howl, the earth may shake, but we continue on a fixed course. The future is always uncertain, but as we look back and count our blessings we can look to the future and know—good times are coming.

Our task is first and foremost to bring the message of Jesus to the world. I am convinced that true change begins in the inner man. If the heart is changed, there will be lasting real change. Then we educate and feed the world.

The new millennium provides opportunities to serve God that were never before possible. Communication by satellite and computers has made us close neighbors to every country of the globe. The prosperity of the developed nations has made our churches strong to finance global Christian activity. Youth fill our churches, the elderly are living longer and better. It is time for the church militant to arise. It is time for every believer to begin to sacrifice time, money and effort to bring about this new golden period. Let us seize the opportunity.

There was a beginning and there will be an end to history. But, that does not mean that our society is closed. Who knows where we will go to from here. The life we enjoy today could not have been conceived just a short 100 years ago, and, who knows what the future holds in scientific discovery, engineering development, in medical breakthroughs and even in social and political harmony? Let us imagine to the fullest and then let us put our ideas into practice. Let us go forward, in the name of Jesus, and change the world.

If you would like to correspond with George DeTellis personally or obtain more information regarding short-term mission opportunities or how to sponsor a child, please write to:

New Missions
P. O. Box 2727
Orlando, Florida 32802

or call:

(407) 240-4058

You can also visit our website

www.newmissions.org

or email:

info@newmissions.org